How It Feels to Be a Child

*the text of this book is printed
on 100% recycled paper*

Books by Carole Klein

THE MYTH OF THE HAPPY CHILD

THE SINGLE-PARENT EXPERIENCE

Carole Klein

How It Feels to Be a Child

Original title: *The Myth of the Happy Child*

HARPER COLOPHON BOOKS

Harper & Row, Publishers

New York, Hagerstown, San Francisco, London

A hardcover edition of this book is published under the title *The Myth of the Happy Child* by Harper & Row, Publishers. Portions of this work originally appeared in *Redbook* and *McCall's*.

HOW IT FEELS TO BE A CHILD. Copyright © 1975 by Carole Klein. All rights reserved. Printed in the United States of America. No part of this book may be used or reproduced in any manner whatsoever without written permission except in the case of brief quotations embodied in critical articles and reviews. For information address Harper & Row, Publishers, Inc., 10 East 53d Street, New York, N.Y. 10022. Published simultaneously in Canada by Fitzhenry & Whiteside Limited, Toronto.

Designed by Dorothy Schmiderer

First HARPER COLOPHON edition published 1977

STANDARD BOOK NUMBER: 06–090550–6

77 78 79 80 81 5 4 3 2 1

For Emily and William Klein,
children I love—people I respect

Contents

Acknowledgments

Before this book officially begins, I want to thank some of the people who helped make it possible. First of course are the boys and girls whose experiences and perceptions so vividly increased my understanding of what it means to be a child. I spoke and listened to great numbers of children in the course of this writing. Many of them you will meet inside these pages. Others, who are less visible, nonetheless provided me with invaluable background material. I wish also to thank the parents of these children, for allowing me to share in their sons' and daughters' lives. A special word of thanks to Ms. Bette Distler, Poet in Residence for the "Project Moppet" program of the Woodbridge Township Public School system in New Jersey. Her students regularly contributed writings to my collection of creative expressions by children about the feelings of childhood.

A word of thanks now to people who figured in a somewhat different way in the development of this book. To Mrs. Barbara Lindeman, a friend and enlightened critic, who never failed to give sharp insights about the material I was exploring. Her questions served to clarify my own thinking, which in turn strengthened my writing.

To my husband, Ted Klein, who provided consistent encouragement and belief that the book would achieve the goals I had set for it.

And finally, to my editor, Mrs. Frances Lindley, whose wise suggestions and range of thinking helped me reach those goals.

CAROLE KLEIN

New York
March 1975

Introduction

Susan, eleven, lies on the hot beach in front of her family's summer home sucking orange soda from a bottle as if the bottle's mouth were covered by a nipple. Her free hand strokes the sand in steady rhythm just as she used to stroke the blanket in her crib. Another child suddenly looms over her and she quickly drops the bottle from her mouth, soda trickling now in orange paths down her cheek. The child makes a jeering comment and tears well up in Susan's eyes as she jumps to her feet. Then, lips still puffy from sucking, she spits in her "friend's" face and runs wildly into the welcome cover of the sea.

Eight-year-old Jimmy dreams that his father pushes him into the washing machine and covers him up with soapy water. Over and over and over he spins around the metal prison, looking out at his father each time his head makes the circle past the window in the front of the machine. His father only smiles at him, seeming not to notice Jimmy's horrible discomfort. The boy wakes up screaming. Still half asleep, he pounds his pillow as if it, not his dream, held him captive. Even after his parents calm him, he refuses to go to sleep unless the door and all the windows to his room are left open.

Bruce comes home from school. The front door is unlocked but his mother isn't there. He runs from empty room to empty room, not able to contain his panic. "Mommy, Mommy, please come out, Mommy!" he screams, throwing open closets, looking under furniture as if he were playing some bizarre version of hide-and-seek. His mother drives up a few minutes later and is horrified at his behavior. She tells him nine-year-old boys don't act this way, and he should be "ashamed" of himself. . . .

He is.

He hangs his head, unable to look at her, but unable also to stop his sobbing. She tells him to go upstairs to his room and "calm down." Meekly he obeys her instructions, and when she follows along just a little bit later, he is asleep—fully dressed, sprawled out on his bed as if hurled there by the force of his emotion. His cheeks are crimson and damply hot with the perspiration of fear.

Bruce and Jimmy and Susan are ordinary children. They have not been introduced to serve as dramatic contrast to what most other children are really like.

("Thank God my Jennifer's not like them!") But of course Jennifer is.

As you follow me through these pages you will meet many children who are very much like your own. Healthy, normal boys and girls who, within that normality, are often extremely happy but often, too, will be quite desolate. A child's world, no matter how much we might like it, cannot be plotted on the map of our illusions: a map that says the landscape of childhood is enchanted, delighted, filled with innocent pleasures and joy. In the vast country of psychic pain, we do not line up in size places. Indeed, evidence now exists that when we have hardly any size at all, we are already learning the conflict attached to being human.

An obstetrician named A. W. Lilly has ascribed a "personality" attribute to a fetus. He believes that the uterus, as softly padded cocoon, doesn't totally protect its developing charge from sensory input. Much of the world outside the mother's womb actually does affect this minuscule pre-person. He will be startled by a sudden noise, hear his mother's heartbeat, is sensitive to her physical restlessness. Experiments show that he responds actively to a needle's touch or the feel of a cold solution. X-rays prove that fetal limbs flail wildly during labor, and that if the baby's head is compressed just a tiny bit during a contraction, its protests are intense and violent. And so the child, it appears, enters his new world already poised for pain, having known its stings as part of the price of being born. And it continues.

The notion of a child's life as idyllic and uncontaminated by significant distress erodes still further in the face of some of these statistics: It has been estimated that on a national level, 10 percent of all children have emotional problems significant enough to warrant professional help. One study of eight hundred elementary school children in a New York suburb, for example, concluded that well over half could have benefited from some form of outside assistance. And these figures fit with disarming neatness into another report by that relentless chronicler of our lives *The New York Times,* which reveals that increasing numbers of children are in fact seeking this assistance. There seems, we are told, little question that the "kiddie on the couch" is more and more a part of the therapeutic scene. Actually, this image is misleading, since few children work out their problems in the traditional horizontal pose. But it's an image that serves to illustrate the report's dramatically contemporary finding. In the years between 1966 and 1971 alone, there was a 63 percent increase in the number of children being treated at a mental health facility. And this startling expansion doesn't include the vast numbers of boys and girls who received some kind of private care.

The rationale behind these statistics varies, with most people feeling that it's the parents' greater sophistication about psychological help that brings the family looking for help. In other words, children are not necessarily more disturbed because they flock in greater numbers than ever before to the therapist's office.

At the same time, the child today, with all his enriched opportunities for experience, has more opportunity for experiencing stress. When asked why this was so, Dr. Robert Traisman, an Illinois psychologist, answered tersely, "Why? Pick up a newspaper!" The doctor then fleshed out his reply, touching in the process all the bases of life's emotional assaults—family tensions, academic pressures, uncertain values and, finally, the fact that we are increasingly a more isolated and "less personal society."

Yet if this book is written to acknowledge that raising a child, especially today, is a worrisome business, it is also written to assert that the stresses a child feels, and yes, many of the effects of stress, lie within the range of what can realistically be called "normal" emotional bruises. So whether outside help is sought or not, there's a larger truth the myth of childhood happiness eclipses: it is incredibly difficult to become a person.

Even with parents' most dedicated efforts to fill their child's life with pleasure, the child will experience many moments of real emotional pain. Anger and fear and loneliness and guilt are only some of the feelings that leap unbidden into children's developing lives. For indeed, they are feelings inevitably connected to growing up.

This inevitability is too often overlooked in the bombardment of material aimed at contemporary parents. The disturbing impression lingers that our slightest blunder will forever maim our child's emotional health. The sight of children "unhappy" fills us, then, not just with loving concern, but with guilt. We remember the too harsh scolding, the preoccupation when we should have been listening, the misreading of signals that totally botched up our ability to meet a need. Surely it was some such behavior that changed the emotional climate. Surely these worries and fears are an index of *our* inadequacy.

It is time to recognize that we often assume unnatural responsibility for feelings natural to the process of growth and development. Certainly we adults are flawed and fallible, as people and as parents, but the reason yesterday's giddily joyous son or daughter now huddles miserably in a chair does not necessarily relate to a particular parental transgression.

Instead these boys and girls are exhibiting behaviors built into their formation as separate people. And however much we ache in empathy for our children's painful feelings, we must acknowledge their right to experience them. Knowing it is not "our fault" will help us do this. We will not have to feel defensive as they make their struggles of self. Understanding the limitations of our ability to change the course of growing up, we can stand by lovingly, ready to offer whatever help we *can* give as they meet the inescapable challenges of childhood.

It is not, I should add now, the purpose of this book to

argue that there is no such thing as emotional illness, or to convince parents that no child will ever find his problems overwhelming. But clearly we live in an age when words like "normal" and "abnormal" must be opened up to a broader range and be judged in a newly relativistic light. Normal for what circumstances? By which person's criteria? As Thomas Szaz says of his profession's own confusion, "Ask six different psychiatrists what 'normal' means and you'll get six totally different answers!"

So nowhere are there agreed-upon definitions. Such uniform thinking belongs to our past, to far more stable times than those we know today. Yet there seems little point in regretting this loss of semantic security. For "stability" as a goal often clothes us in strait jackets, narrowing the life space so much that only our steady breaths provide any excitement. Bruno Bettelheim, that veteran of child-raising, refers to this dulled image of the "good" life when he says: "high on my list of priorities for childrearing in the future is to correct the current fallacy that it's desirable to rear children who are insulated from the frustrations and difficulties of life . . . we must teach them from childhood on that the success of living is in the ability to meet the difficulties; to struggle through."

I remembered this when I read the report of psychologist Morris Hymowitz about yet another study. This time it involved nearly two thousand boys, followed over a twelve-year period, revealing at study's end only fifty who showed no visible signs of any psychopathology. Dr. Hymowitz's addendum to the report supports Dr. Bettelheim's belief that yes, perhaps struggling through is more important than fitting in. For even as I wonder, awe-struck, what kind of soil this tiny elite group of fifty was nurtured in—even as I nervously speculate if I could ever develop a similar green thumb with my own children—I am told that the uniquely stable handful of trouble-free children were also "lacking in imagination and creativity, and were highly limited in their interests and activities." The calmness I am inclined to covet seemed also to spell passivity and dully repetitive behavior.

Incredible! The impossible dream, attained, brings only yawns. Nonetheless, despite such challenges to our innocence, even with enormous holes rent in the illusion that any time of life, as we know life today, can be paradise, we still hope *our* children will have childhoods of innocent contentment.

It is such a hope that often tempts us to renovate reality. So mothers will pick up their children from school (perhaps after their own regular analysts' appointments) and smile benignly at each other as they watch the play and listen to the shrieks and laughter. That a boy leans against the wall only watching, that a girl hunches her shoulders in mortified awareness of developing breasts, that a child still smarts from the sharp sarcasm of a teacher, that invitations to a birthday party leave uninvited children feeling marked as lepers—this the mothers too often do not (will not?) see.

There is a particular dynamic to this myopia—what no less an authority on man's lopsided eyesight than Sigmund Freud referred to as "childhood amnesia." As the phrase quite simply and powerfully suggests, it is difficult to understand a child's world because it is impossible to recall what our own world, in childhood, was truly like. For when we look back at our own early pasts, we don't so much remember as reconstruct. I who remember am not the person I am remembering. I am an adult woman, with scars and fears, with needs and interests and goals far different from those I had when I was four or six or even fourteen. Yes, of course, I can remember events out of the past—chronological signposts that thread through the years, tying together significant times in my life—but I cannot feel the climate of the country that I traveled.

So I can say to my child, "I remember how it felt not to be invited to a birthday party," but the fact is I do *not* remember. Yes, I can recall rejection similar to what she experiences now, but I cannot in empathy touch her aching soreness, for it is, after all, only the event I recall and not its emotional essence.

Even the most vivid childhood memories are only fragments, half-truths that don't tell the whole story of who I once was. I can tell you that I remember being critically ill when I was four years old. And I even catch sight of my father, dressed in a leather jacket and a woolen cap because the windows all had to be open despite the frigid weather to aid my breathing. But I cannot tell you through the retrospective blur how it felt to lie in bed trying to breathe, or how it felt to me to have him there beside me. I don't know what expressions ranged across his face: love, or anger, or fear— or how those nonverbal communications were heard by me. My own adult truth submerges the truth of that child in bed, and she remains, in ways that matter, a stranger.

Psychiatrist Ernest Schachtel, an authority on memory, says that "even the most profound and prolonged psycho-analysis does not lead to a recovery of childhood memory; at best it unearths some incidents and feelings that had been forgotten."

Emphasis here is on the word "some," as the doctor's use of it is particularly significant in this age of analytic encounter. For no matter how earnestly we try, no matter how often or expensively we pour out our pasts to a "significant other," the past remains shrouded by the accumulated experiences and repressions of our developing selves.

Repression is, as indicated, the powerfully resistant factor in childhood amnesia. In countless ways we're taught to deny those aspects of ourselves that don't fit in with family and cultural values. We are tamed, inhibited, trained to be part of society's machinery. By the time we're adults, we've learned the mechanics of the machine too well. We don't carry with us, from those earlier selves, responses that go against the people we've become. The intense emotional experiencing of a child's world is out of place in this no-nonsense, achievement-oriented, grown-up world we now call home. And so when we look at children, they are quaintly foreign—visitors from another country, even though their country was once our own.

Schachtel explains neatly: "Childhood amnesia covers those aspects and experiences of the former personality which are incompatible with the culture."

It of course has always been true that adults and children have faced each other across the divide of time as long as they have coexisted. But as with so many other aspects of living, it's the same, only more so, today. If adults historically haven't been able to identify with what a child really feels, they could at least identify with his patterns of growth and development. After all, a child moved pretty well through the same tunnel to adulthood as had his parents, placing his feet in paths well marked by those who had come this way before. At the end of the tunnel, light shone on a world equally pretested and familiar. He would be a grownup, like his parents.

But he is very, very different from his parents, this child

today. Margaret Mead, a lady who has watched several generations from several worlds come through the tunnel, compares contemporary parents and children to what happens when a tribe in New Guinea is suddenly "exposed to airplanes and transistor radios," or when "children of cannibals go away to medical school."

The analogy is graphically apt, if jarring to urbane self-concepts. Despite martinis and master's degrees, we are in many ways primitives when compared to our children. The frame of reference for us to share is uncomfortably limited.

A child grows up and into a world assaulted with a technology that is massive, and with massive implications for how he *views* the world. From television to the bomb to space travel, he's the product of an age that raises questions his parents never dreamed of, and defies answers they may have built a life by. There is often a widening discrepancy, as the child grows, between his parents' "truth" and that of the world outside. His parents say one thing, his experience another—creating a kind of confusion children have never quite felt before. How to make sense of it . . . ? Where are the guidelines?

Dr. Mead comments, "No one, teachers, physicians, parents, knows anything about dealing with the child who [is] someone they will never be, and about whom we can make no prediction," adding to that, lest we not get her message, ". . . we have no idea at all what the world is going to be like 40 years from now."

So, to a startlingly new degree, a child today is at the center of his own "becoming." It has always been difficult, painful, profoundly wrenching to make life coherent, but now it is particularly hard.

Knowing this, my response deepens to a girl named Greta,

who is a child you'll meet often as this book unfolds. Greta is six, youngest child in a family with three boys. She has long brown hair and a dimple that sits higher on her cheek than any dimple I've ever seen, just at the top of her cheekbone, so that when she smiles it seems to point the way to her eyes, their deep brown color so appropriate to their sloping almond shape.

Today there are tears in Greta's eyes. She'd had a troubled night, bad dreams that reflected a plaguing discomfort about the challenges of first grade.

"I wish," she said finally, tears spilling over now, "I wish I knew . . . *everything!* If I knew everything, I could"—she takes a deep breath, and scales the heights of her despair, and comes up with the ultimate conquering of experience's peak —"I could sleep with the lights out!"

It seems to me—and hence the reason for this book—that the only way to help Greta sleep with the lights out is to turn them on in the many rooms of her childhood. Understanding the experiences the rooms contain will help us understand Greta. And in seeing her, and all our children, as the people they really are, we can help them escape the tyranny of imposed perceptions of what they're "supposed" to be.

I am what I am
Don't make me be what I'm not
Because . . .
It won't be me.
                    —BETH (age 10)

To me it seems that youth is, like
spring, an over-praised season . . .
more remarkable, as a general rule,
for biting east winds, than genial
breezes.
                    —SAMUEL BUTLER

How It Feels to Be a Child

1 / The Myth
and Its Effects

A child breaks a toy and cries as if his heart also lay in scattered pieces. We soothe him briefly and then, when the crying continues, push him (however gently, it *is* a push) aside . . . ready ourselves to move on to more important tasks.

We snap at a child who hangs around the kitchen after school, refusing to go out to play because "nobody likes me."

"You have lots of friends," we assure him briskly, and send him on his way. Later, when he comes home clearly wounded by rejection, we accuse him of deliberately not having a good time. Our anger rises with surprising swiftness and we treat his sadness as though it were a flimsy, inappropriate costume—not the real clinging cloth of his experience.

Nancy is ten. She is small-boned and fragile-looking. Her thick hair, which she wears in one long dark braid, appears too heavy for her rather tiny face. The hair seems to belong to someone older and stronger. When you first look at her, your vision seems almost to divide—first the face and then the hair, the contrast too sharp to have fused yet into one image. Interestingly, this is almost a metaphor for Nancy's personality. She is, her mother sighs in frustration, like two people. The oldest of three children, she sometimes seems the youngest. Her moods are volatile, buffeting her equilibrium and that of everyone else around. In the middle of a crying, kicking tantrum, she may run out to the garden and pull up all the flowers, jumping up and down on them until they're thickly perfumed dust.

Or she will literally tremble with fear over some "tiny" event. A simple quiz in school, a new baby-sitter due for an evening. Her body shakes and her voice catches in her throat when she tries to tell her mother what it is that has suddenly created her spreading panic.

And then, at other times, she's as wise as though she had lived for many years beyond her actual ten. When I talk to her during such periods, I can completely forget, in the intellectual meeting, that this is according to any calendar a child. She has the rare ability to strike directly to the bone of a situation—sizing it up and wrapping it up with no string of pretense left hanging. For example, when we were talking about some mother in the neighborhood who considers herself a playmate of her children, Nancy was unimpressed. Yes, she agreed, the woman did sometimes go sleigh-riding and roller-skating with her daughter, and did make the most elaborate birthday parties of any of her friends, but, said Nancy, "that's just doing, not being. Anyway, if I were her kid, I'd always have a stomach ache. It's like she starves you when she doesn't feel like feeding you, and then she stuffs you full of things when she wants to show off her cooking."

Last summer, thinking it might help strike a balance between the babyishness and grown-up sensitivity, Nancy's parents sent her to camp. Predictably, letters covered the range of her personality—sometimes lyrically enthused, often perceptive, occasionally poetically unhappy.

A note dashed off quickly before a play rehearsal, filled with proud excitement about her starring role, would be followed by: "Counselors aren't much different than teachers. They treat you like you're a lump of clay. . . . They like little statue people, not real kids." Or: "I was very, very homesick yesterday. It made me feel like an old lady sitting on a broken bench with her mouth closed."

On visiting day at camp, Nancy's parents barely drove up to the gate before she hurled herself out from behind it and threw herself into their arms. It was clear from her sunflushed face that she had been watching for them for hours.

The force of her greeting was overwhelming. As Nancy's mother untangled herself from the embrace, she said with a little laugh, "You couldn't have missed us all that much!" And before Nancy could insist she had, her father showed her the treats they had brought, snacks and games and comic books, pulling them out of the bag as though they were objects of seduction. There was an edge of tension, almost palpable, to the scene, as the parents looked around, self-consciously gauging the relative drama of other family reunions.

If the children in this book are all "normal" children, the parents are all "normal" parents—men and women who don't go out of their way to ignore their sons' and daughters' pain. Neither are they all uniquely insensitive people who, because they have never felt what their children feel, can't begin to understand what it means to be hurt, or frightened, or lonely.

No, it is precisely because we ourselves often know these emotions all too well that we avert our eyes from the truth of childhood. As suggested, it is the harsh reality of adult life that deepens the need to believe in myth. Relentlessly disappointed, we want our children to be hopeful. Disillusioned with love, we hope our children never question love's benevolence. Cheated by the false rewards of acquisition, we delight in our child's eager sense of promise.

Similarly, since it sometimes seems that the more we learn, the more we see life's absurdities, we find a child's "naïve" approach to experience enchanting. . . .

"When I'm with a bad baby-sitter, I don't come out of my room all night," says six-year-old, ever articulate Robert—flaming red hair, perfect nose, huge blue eyes sketching myth's child (anxiety about abandonment, plaguing bad dreams, ever present fear of failure—in spite of dramatically high IQ—making him very much reality's child). "Why don't you come out?" I ask him, and he tells me, "Because this way, I can say she's not there."

Judy, a chubby five-year-old—new to kindergarten, hating the walk to school every day because she's the smallest child on the block and is sure the "big third-graders" are laughing at her (many times she's right)—understands exactly what Robert is saying. She confesses a "secret"—that lots of times she walks all the way to school with her eyes closed. I had noticed, and like Judy's mother been puzzled by, the unusual number of bruises on her legs. Now it was explained. Eyes screwed tight, she kept bumping into telephone poles and garbage cans while she walked. But it was a fate she preferred to a visual collision with what she perceived as towering menaces to her newly emerging independent self.

In our envy of the child's apparent belief that he can erase what he'd rather not see, we recognize neither the confusion that requires an eraser nor the shadow that always remains, stubbornly resisting the rub. Judy's fear doesn't disappear because she won't focus on its source. It is only temporarily dimmed. Yes, Judy and Robert through their make-believe can detoxify reality to some degree. Indeed, with the limited powers of childhood, pretending is often the only way *to* deal with unpleasant situations. But ironically the situations may be perceived as far more unpleasant than they actually are. And it is this truth that should keep us from being wistfully amused by the naïveté behind barricaded door and eyes squeezed closed.

Obviously neither the baby-sitter nor the third-graders are real physical threats. But for a variety of reasons (many of which are discussed in the chapter on fears) they are perceived as threats. In the same way, the interplay of all experience is given a subjective as well as an objective reading by the child trying to make sense of the characters and plots in his expanding life. What *seems* to be happening is frequently as real as what actually *is* happening. Down through the ages, adults have said in horrified wonder to parents become less awesome, "But I always thought you disapproved of me," or "thought I was dumb," or "preferred" a brother or sister.

Yet so real were some of those pains when they happened that they probably shaped our lives, influenced the decisions we made, the directions we took. Therefore, when Greta says to me one morning, her voice bleak, "Daddy took my brothers to his office," I hear in her voice and read in her face total and utter rejection. And even though I know her father adores her, I am sure her unhappiness is, in this moment, real.

When we talk, there's an outpouring of evidence about why she was deliberately left behind. Her brothers are smarter, Daddy can play ball with them, she spills her milk all the time—a litany of grievances against herself. She shuffles her sandal on and off her foot, not looking at me, refusing in head-down mumbling to accept my suggestion that she talk to her father and tell him how much she would like to visit his office too. Maybe, I say rather desperately, knowing it is true, he just doesn't realize how much it means to her.

Eyes still fixed on her jiggling shoe, she answers me, her voice so low that I have to strain to hear it:

"I did say something, and he said I wouldn't have anything to do there all day. He said someday he'll take me when he has time for us to go out to a movie or something. . . . It's okay," she says then, and I'm chilled by her way of closing down conversation. "It's okay. . . . I didn't want to go anyway."

I am chilled because I see in Greta's response what R. D. Laing has called the "politics of experience." By this he means that in a family there is a "power struggle" over whose perception of an experience will be called real. Parents needing the order of a quiet evening, for example, decide a child is sleepy, so he'll go off to bed in spite of the fact that his body feels not the least little bit fatigued. The myth of happy childhood perpetuates this pattern of separating a child from his real experiencing. For it helps adults guiltlessly accept their own arguments.

Greta's father, believing that he has a happy little girl, who certainly is always sure of being loved, can keep his day less complicated by not having to amuse her. He tells himself, and can believe it, that she wouldn't have a good time in his office. Needing her father's love (which she is not at *all* sure of), Greta tries to believe it too. The myth prevails as she kisses him good-by without further complaint. But in the process, she has taken one more step toward self-estrangement; has sacrificed one more piece of her autonomy on the altar of approval.

Aggrandizing the myth and the child's inherent helplessness "excuses" adult self-righteousness. It allows us to justify, as Greta's father did, the restrictions and repressing dictums we inevitably lay down on children. After all, the helpless need protection. They must be told whom to trust, and taught how to behave so that the world accepts, not rejects, them. And we do want the world to accept them.

For we are, however unhappy in the job, licensed franchisers of that world. Generations of parents have gathered their children around society's counter and enticed them to buy, even as they themselves did, what Nancy referred to as "little statue people"—replicas of what the culture thinks they should be. "Adjust," we nervously say, "fit in, conform. . . . Here—accept these imperatives. No, no—repress those impulses."

The urgency stems from increasing uncertainty about where we ourselves fit in. Therefore, not just in my child's successful adherence to rules, but in his smiling face as he follows them, lies, I think, my own redemption. A happy child is evidence I'm doing my work well. Anxiety about my role and function is soothed. What have I accomplished in life? Well, look right here—I have a happy child!

Understandably, then, when the child broods, and attacks, or is frightened, he frightens me. For divergence from the myth of happiness also carries implications of a parent's failure. If my child is *not* happy, as the myth says he should be, then something I did or didn't do has caused his "atypical" pain.

Is it any wonder, then, that many parents, like Judy's, try

to shut their eyes to behavior that might if really confronted cause *them* pain?

In the study mentioned earlier, where it was concluded that a large proportion of the eight hundred children being observed could have benefited from professional help, it was also concluded that the reason they rarely got the help was because parents resisted the idea it was needed. Largely inappropriate feelings of responsibility for what was "going wrong" made mothers and fathers bury their heads in the sand while they insisted everything was all right.

Inevitably this no-news-is-good-news, what-I-can't-see-won't-hurt-me approach to the real experiencing of childhood often leaves children in lonely possession of their discomfort. As we saw with Greta, very early in life, long before they learn to read, they begin learning the scripts of what they perceive as being "acceptable" expressions of self. When Nancy's parents came to camp, they whirled through the day in circles of distraction from her unhappiness. They took her to the most coveted local restaurant for lunch, participated with genuine glee in all her camp activities, were wildly enthusiastic about even her smallest triumph. But as surely as if they had bound and gagged her, they made it impossible for her to communicate what she was really feeling. With their love for her undisputed, their obsession with producing a happy child turned the spigot to "off" for any expression of emotional pain.

Study after study proves that children sense what feelings are unacceptable to their parents and carefully edit them out of their meetings. Little boys, for example, whose fathers cling to the machismo image do not, no matter how loving they are with their fathers, talk about being afraid to play ball. And Nancy's plaintive comment, as her parents drove away, that "Mommy doesn't like me to be sad" paints a smile on her face while she waves good-by, even though tears flow silently inside. Dr. Irving Markowitz, who heads a major family service agency in the New York area, says that in a sense, children in these situations are being asked to be their "parents' therapist." The child creates an almost analytic encounter, assessing his parents' needs and calming their self-doubt by steering their relationship in the need's direction. But, says Dr. Markowitz, children when they do this are "faking" childhood. And it is never comfortable to breathe behind a mask, no matter how cheerfully smiling it may be.

Obsession with happiness slaps masks not only on children but on ourselves as well. Our eagerness to keep them "happy" paints confusingly cheerful faces over tearful experience. When Jimmy's grandmother died, he was "protected" from seeing any real expression of grief. As if she were in the middle of sex, his mother guiltily arranged her emotions whenever he entered the room.

"He never saw me cry once," she says proudly, adding in sighing explanation of her self-denial, "After all, he has time enough to know how much it hurts to lose a person you love." But I wonder—and it's not an idle question—will he really be able to deal with loss, or with love, when that time comes? Dr. Markowitz reflects the views of many of his colleagues who, like himself, make archaeological digs into patients' long-calcified feelings, when he explains that we serve as models for our children's emotional life. So that in "denying that the death of someone we love is such a terrible loss, we are implying that no relationship should ever be taken too deeply."

In such an antiseptic emotional climate, the air grows thin, the depth of experience runs shallow. Surely this is not a very meaningful heritage for any child. Yet guilt because the myth isn't working causes the most loving parents to deny children perhaps their most meaningful inheritance—the right to total possession of the fullest spectrum of their feelings.

2 / The Argument Against the Myth

If this book questions the mythology of childhood, it clings to believing in its miracles. The imagination is stunned at the idea that this writhing newborn infant sleeps under a blanket made from the history of the world. Yet generations of ancestors have passed on their genetic story, now to be told by him.

Skeptical though we are of old moralities that made sex and procreation a holy sacrament, the joining of sperm and egg seems, even in its admitted randomness, miraculous. Why that particular night's union and not another?

So it's still awesome to think that this tiny ball of instincts and movements was only nine months ago a single cell. What we may not know in our initial confrontation is that nine months from now, we'll be even more awe-struck when those infant movements will have already been incorporated into countless numbers of complex skills—each one making the child more aware of himself as a developing person.

He will, for example, no longer lie inertly in his crib, but instead will frequently grasp at things outside it, exploring with the excitement of first discovery their newness and special meaning. Some objects will particularly please the senses, like soft toys and bottles filled with warm milk. And he can perceive differences and make associations between animate and inanimate objects. The puppy that dances on the animal mobile above his crib swings back into position after he pokes it with his fists; the family dog runs yelping from the room at a similar prod through crib bars. So, too, the child begins to attach different emotional meanings to his perceptions. Only a live puppy is capable of licking his face in affection, and only the living animal's heartbeat under his hand can be so comforting.

A child is the center of his world, but the world expands continuously as he grows. When he pulls himself to his feet in his playpen, his life has radically changed. He now stands like other human beings, alongside them and opposite them, and can begin to get a wider sense of himself as a person who shares the experience of life and being human.

All this is the process of becoming a person—the story of how an infant gradually grows into full membership in society. And the process is, by its very definition, part one of the three-part argument against the myth of the always happy child. For it tells us that childhood is *developmental*. And because this means "becoming," rather than "being," the sands continuously shift underfoot, with no steady spot to nurture the contentment known through security. Yes, as a child whirls in the dizzying dance of developmental change, there may certainly be peaks of incredible joy, but they cannot be counted on to last. The calendar's turn into another growth period plummets him crazily to the tilting ground. Ground that is cold now where yesterday it was warm, hard and rough now where it was recently lush and rich.

The growth of a person involves far more than learning to

speak and walk and grasp widening sets of techniques. As he moves through the stages of physical development, the child experiences that development, experiences his world in ways unique to him.

Unfortunately, his uniqueness is frequently not recognized, which is one of the pieces of evidence in development's case against contentment. For although there are patterns of growth—babbling before speech, crawling before walking—the trip is not the same for all travelers through childhood. No matter how many charts are drawn about developmental curves and average behavior, a particular child cannot totally be captured by statistics. So the idea that all young passengers should be at a particular developmental place at a designated time leaves too many children breathlessly trying to catch up, more convinced with each frustrated effort that they'll always be lagging behind. They strain at the uniform of childhood, longing for some right to variation in its design. Rarely is it given. Like some mass-produced quartermaster's stock, identical clothing is issued to meet the turbulent weather of childhood's real climate.

For this reason, impressively bright Robert comes home from first grade in hot-faced humiliation, painfully sharing his "stupidness" over not being able to master the small muscle control six-year-olds are "supposed" to have, the better to tie shoelaces without teacher's help.

It's important to remember that the objective turmoil of development is always influenced by the subjective emotional perception of experience. Events and interactions and exchanges filter past a screen through which the child "feels" what is happening, even as he takes part in the happening itself. Therefore, if enough six-year-olds in the classroom *can* tie their shoes, and if the teacher cares enough about the accomplishment, Robert's trailing shoelaces can indeed form the word "stupid" for all, but most of all for himself in self-contempt, to see.

What a child sees in his personal mirror is very much influenced by what Harry Stack Sullivan called the "reflected appraisals" of other people. So Robert looks in the mirror and sees his physical self. But how he and children in general evaluate that self relates in large part to how significant people in their lives have judged their reflection. Too often it's the other person's perception that shapes their own—the other person's truth that comes perilously close to being the truth.

While parents are the most significant people in most children's lives, other people also have a great deal to do with how they see themselves—other people like, for instance, teachers.

In research on the forming of self-concepts, school weighs heavily on the scale of both positive and negative developing perceptions. One study of children from elementary school through college age had a quarter of the respondents referring to school as a factor in what they liked or didn't like about themselves. And it should be quickly added that the bulk of these responses showed school a much more fertile ground for nurturing self-contempt than self-esteem. Its towering certainties about what children are supposed to be make children feel even more inadequate and helpless about what in their chaotic development they really are. It's no wonder that fantasy about school often reflects a sense of powerlessness and the eager wish for magical gifts of strength. . . .

"If I were magic," recites Judy, "I would turn every school into a big, big pile of ants. But they'd still be ants so they'd be tiny and so I would be much more bigger and I would jump up and down and jump up and down until they were squashed in a dirty lumpy pile." She finishes breathlessly. Then, as I'm about to speak, she turns and adds a finishing fillip: "And then I'd take off my shoes and scrunch the school dirt in my toes and wash it off in the shower so it all ran down the drain." This last image sends her into peals of giggles, a raucous level of gaiety I have heard only when formerly religious friends tell some ultimately blasphemous joke.

So powerful a force can school be in a child's response to his own development that it can even take precedence over the family's more sympathetic atmosphere. Robert's mother laughs and kisses him when he confesses his morning's failure. "Who cares about such a silly thing?" she asks gaily. "I promise you: by the time you go to college you'll know how to tie your shoes." Robert tries a smile to match her own, but what his mother doesn't know is that in his weakened self-regard, as surely as Robert knows his name he knows that the boy named Robert will never be smart enough to go to college.

No; just because there's evidence to support adult measurements of a situation—this is a "big deal," that's only a "little thing"—it still doesn't mean very much to the child caught in the hurricane center of his feelings, who continues to wrestle with the subjective aspects of his experience. Picture eight-year-old Jimmy, for example, who finds his wiry but undersized body shameful. His friends are all bigger, often stronger, able to reach higher in basketball games and jump broader hurdles in gym class. Jimmy's parents understand his distress, although they don't share it because they know, and tell him, that everyone in their family is just a "slow grower." And indeed Jimmy's father grazes six feet, and his older brother gained nearly a foot when he hit adolescence. So see, Jimmy, they say consolingly, you'll "catch up" with your friends later on.

But catching up isn't the same as being equal now. And Jimmy, in childhood, is rooted in now, although many negative perceptions he forms about himself will affect his self-view for years to come. In the same way that studies show fat children "feel" obese long after they've become really thin, physical characteristics that a child is unhappy with, like shortness, can distort the self-image even when his head is clearly lintel instead of only table high.

Even when a child doesn't feel distressingly "different," he will feel that the mirror of developing self is at times the mirror of an unfunny fun house. Periodically it distorts the image he expects and wants to see. For the real point is that the image isn't fixed. No child can say "This is who I am" and have a reasonable sense of confidence that when he looks again he will recognize whom he sees. Inevitably, in the spinning physical and emotional and intellectual changes of development, the person in the mirror will sometimes be a stranger. It will be a person whose responses you can't count on, or in any way predict.

In all stages of growth, including those labeled particularly peaceful, like the years before real adolescence, lifting the label always shows some very untranquil developmental activity. Many of the ten- and eleven-year-olds, and certainly the twelve- and thirteen-year-olds I dealt with proved to me that their conflicts, however well concealed, had by no means ceased to exist. Much of their trouble had to do with the total newness of their experiencing. The steps they were taking away from childhood and into adolescence were so tentative, so experimental. There was no history to support a feeling or response, let alone a bravely taken action.

For some children the mirror's unsteady reflection can bring particular pain. Again, so much of the unhappy response relates to a discrepancy between what they would like to be physically and what they actually see they are. Children like Susan, eleven, whose bulky body is a body she agonizes over endlessly, can work herself up to frenzies of despair over both her inner and outer image. The still shapeless contours (will they ever be otherwise? she wonders) of her flesh are only matched in the self-hating pain they provoke by the unwelcome shapes of feeling inside her head, currents of chaos that sweep her along till she sometimes loses control.

One morning recently she spent forty-five minutes changing and rechanging her clothes for school. The blouse worn outside makes her look "pregnant"; the blouse tucked in declares her lack of a waistline; the body shirt pulls at her stomach and accentuates the deficiencies of her totally nonaccented chest; the sweater stops just at her hips, outlining their width. Each outfit makes her face more flushed, her eyes more damp. Each outfit gets thrown in furious rejection onto the bed, wrinkling the pile of clothes already bitterly discarded.

Finally she leaves for school, knowing as she bolts from her mother's annoyance because she hasn't eaten breakfast that her mother will soon be furious at the sight of her bedroom, and that the anger will be waiting for her at three o'clock. She knows, too, that hunger will, as her mother predicts, take over the morning and knows what her mother doesn't know: that its pangs will relentlessly call her attention to the body she hates now with such total passion.

Later that morning, Susan comes to our writing class. She seems lethargic and doesn't participate in any discussion. But when the class is over, she hands me this poem.

THE MEANING OF BEING ME

Who Am I? Who Am I?
Growing up isn't easy, no matter what you think.
No. No. It's hard. It's hard.
It's standing on the brink
of a mountain that
    you're afraid of.
    Sometimes I ask you who I am, but you don't tell me.
    Sometimes I ask myself who I am. . . .
Still a kid?
Soon a grown-up person. (Will it be better then?
Can you tell me that . . . can I believe it?)
I hear a certain song and I get
  tears in my eyes. . . .
I see a person and I get so angry—and he never even
  said a word. . . .
It's hard, growing up . . . it's so hard. Why must it
  be so hard. . . .
The littlest rough spot and there I go—crying,
angry . . . up to my room to break down—to kick—to have
  bad dreams—
I hurt you, and you, and you, sometimes—but I hurt me
  more times.
I don't want to hurt you, and I don't want to hurt me—
But it hurts so much not to know
  how to answer,
Who am I?

Susan would not show this poem to her mother at the time she wrote it although her mother would certainly have empathized with its turmoil. Instead she burrowed deeper into her misery, made worse now by isolation. Worry about what she is "supposed" to feel frequently keeps Susan from the comfort of sharing her feelings. It is a worry that relates to the second argument against the myth—the overwhelming *dependency* that is the counterpoint rhythm of childhood. From the time he lies in his bed hungry, needing someone else to bring food to make hunger disappear, dependency for his emotional and physical survival encircles a child. As he grows, his awareness of his continuing inadequacy imposes false fronts on instinctual responses and feelings. For he must, he feels, please the people whose care he needs, even those whom he would perhaps like to defy but is not yet strong enough to.

Take Nancy, for instance, who generally puts her "best" face forward in school, and is approvingly labeled by all her teachers as extremely "cooperative." On her last report card the teacher wrote, as if she were bestowing a gift, "Nancy is a delight. She never fails to do what is asked or expected of her." But in one of our writing groups, we play a metaphor game, and this same blandly yes-saying child writes, in a resentment undimmed by its neat lettering and perfect spelling: "I am a new house with no locks on my doors—everyone walks into my rooms without knocking."

Actually Nancy has created an analogy that describes with chilling accuracy what children's lives are often like. The invasion of privacy inflicted on a child is great and, often, the act of adults who have the most sincere respect for other people's rights. We do shove the Nancys and the Roberts and all the other growing selves called children into unlocked rooms, where paradoxically they're kept prisoner by our constant surveillance. They have no way to keep us from barging in at random whim, usually to teach another variation of socialization's favorite game—learning "right" from "wrong." We tell them what to do, how to act, what to think, and even how to look. The battle over hair and dress imposes grown-up taste on a child's developing one—and his need for our approval encourages him to "understand" that ours is the only "right" one.

That there's so little resistance to this dominating intrusion relates to fear of what lies outside childhood's unrespected perimeters. To one standing on the world's sidelines, the action in the center can seem pretty grim. It's a world that seems essentially an unfriendly place, with evil perhaps lurking, as in Hansel and Gretel, behind every falsely welcoming door.

Ask a child why there are rules and laws, and he'll tell you somberly, as four-year-old, darkly handsome George told me, "so that people don't go around killing and robbing each other."

What kind of people? I ask. "Everybody," he answers, obviously surprised at the silliness of my question. Don't tell *him* about internal control. Much realer chains keep all our villainy in line. Even when they're considerably older than George, this life view persists. Without rules, children imply, man's basic meanness would blossom. Left to people's own judgment, justice rarely would reign. This wild-garden view of life, a far cry from the mythic, gently flowering idea of how a child thinks, increases children's worries about their helplessness.

So it is their sense of inadequacy, not hostile malevolence, that provokes a discussion like the one between Greta and her mother when they were caught in a sudden snowstorm. During the frighteningly slippery automobile trip home, Greta asked worriedly about the possibility of their having an accident. Her mother started to say something reassuring about the lack of real danger, but Greta waved away the answer. She clearly wanted to get to the heart of the issue. What if, she asked, they have an accident and her mother is killed. Who will take Greta home? The questions continued —grotesque background for the harrowing ride.

Will Daddy be able to really take care of her—make her lunch and braid her hair? Does he know where her piano teacher lives, and will he be too strict about homework?

With heroic composure, her mother answered all the questions, drawing the lines of security tighter back around the child, so that finally she was satisfied. Humming a favorite song, Greta sat back in the seat, while her mother told herself silently that self-fulfilling prophecies don't really come from six-year-olds.

The excessively intense relationships within the nuclear family contribute to the problems children today have with dependency. Margaret Mead has written that with only two people to give security, a child always lives with the anxiety that one will disappear, leaving him with a meager half loaf only. This is quickly obvious when you work with children in writing about their worries and feelings. Family "fights" are mentioned over and over as threats to emotional well-being. . . .

"Arguments always scare me," writes eight-year-old Cathy. "I'd even rather my mother got mad at *me* than at my father."

"I get so scared when my father doesn't come home from work on time," Robert tells me, "but it's worse when Mommy yells at him when he does come home."

And ten-year-old Andy, whose outside self—all athletic skills and muscular build and jutting chin—belies the poet who lives inside, says that if he were invisible, "I would seal my mother's mouth with honey so that when she talked to my father all her words would sound sweet because they had to push out through the honey before he heard them!"

Many psychiatrists I talked with believed that the nuclear family's dependency forces a child into unfortunately narrowed experiments with self-fulfillment, for his fear of losing these exclusive sources of security makes him behave only in ways that are sure to win parental approval. And the sad fact is we do engage in a kind of trade-off with our children's dependency. It's the rare parent who doesn't exploit a child's need for approval and love in order to shape his behavior. The kiss or the spank become symbols of love or rejection, and when one is needed so badly, and the other is feared so terribly, they far outweigh their superficial significance.

"I don't understand what he's making such a fuss about," Dougie's mother says in embarrassed exasperation. With three-year-old curiosity (and competition for the attention I was receiving), Dougie had emptied all the drawers in the living room. The sight of playing cards, coasters, rubber-bands, tissues, toothpicks and cocktail napkins piled into messy collage had moved my friend to grab her son and lay a not very heavy hand to his bottom. Fortunately, they live in a private house, for surely in an apartment the screams would have alerted neighbors to a child's being battered on the other side of the wall. And indeed, in a way, Dougie was feeling battered by his mother's anger. His own walls of security were suddenly crumbling, admitting strong gusts of wind he well knew he couldn't resist on his own. Later, when his mother hugged and kissed him and wiped away the burning tears, the walls were solid again, protecting him from experiences he couldn't at this point in his development handle by himself.

Critics of our style of socialization call such giving and

taking of affection "anxiety conditioning," meaning exactly what the phrase implies. Children often learn to be "good" because there's so much anxiety involved in being "bad." A conditioned response gets attached to a forbidden action and not only precludes taking the action but makes the idea behind it, in effect, unthinkable. To allow the thought or feeling or impulse is to go against the guidelines for keeping love. Better stay within them while you try to make sense of your developing life.

And it is often so hard to make sense of it all. . . . A long time ago, the philosopher Descartes crawled into a stove to puzzle the mystery of man. At the end of the day, when he climbed out, he said, "I think, therefore I am." Children in a way reverse this tale. Their inability really to understand and clarify their thoughts makes it hard for them to grab hold of the meaning of their lives. Delicately blond Cathy writes, in our metaphor game, "I am a cloud. . . . I drift around in the sky and never really know where I am." And Jimmy, who first uses his despised shortness as the core of his self-concept, saying, "I'm a forty-five record. . . . My music always shuts off before anyone listens," later dictates, "It's really hard to describe me. I think that maybe if I tried I could, but what could I really say? I'm happy that you want to hear my feelings, but I wish you could come inside my head and sort them out first." And then he adds, as if I, this omnipotent grownup, could really see inside his head and he'd better protect himself, ". . . but I don't want you to tell out loud what you find." Jimmy's belief that I can see and tell him who he is indicates the *cognitive confusion* that is the final third of the argument against the myth of the happy child. For intellectual development is also still in process and this means that children will frequently gain the approval they need so badly by behaving in ways whose logic totally escapes them.

"I want it!" Dougie wails when his mother takes back a truck he's pulled from another child's hand. He is told it doesn't matter that he wants it—it "belongs" to someone else. He is told in simply stated words but a highly serious tone of voice about property rights and asking for permission. And all the while his eyes are fixed on the shiny red wonder of the truck, and his hand fairly tingles with the remembered tactile joy of it, ready as it was to be pushed in careening pleasure across the room. He reminds me of an alcoholic being given a temperance lecture in a liquor store; and I feel his bewilderment at having to sacrifice immediate gratification for concepts that can have no real meaning at this stage in his intellectual development.

The point is that, at three, a truck in hand is much more meaningful than any strength of character attainable through resisting temptation. Just as it's "better" to eat with your face right over your plate when the food smells so good that way. Just as when I whisper to George to lower his voice while he criticizes his sitter, he is clearly puzzled. Why should he deny what he's genuinely feeling in the name of some abstract principle of social behavior? Indeed, when I ask children to list questions they have about "rules," they pour out as from buckets of bewilderment so vast there isn't any seeable bottom. Why be nice to people you don't like? . . . Why take baths when you don't mind being dirty? . . . Why clean up your toys if you don't mind the clutter? . . . Why not interrupt people when you have something to say? . . . Why not cry when you're hurt, or kick when you're angry, or be nasty to the teacher or sitter if she's nasty to you? . . .

Long into childhood this confusion exists. Until obedience gives way to understanding, a child feels the distress of being outside his experiencing, the puzzled observer of his own behavior. The linkage between possessing your life and possessing your ideas is very real, and the emotional pain until that linkage is forged is also, and awfully, real.

So real that if he's sufficiently perplexed a child may box himself into an even tinier corner of experience than childhood normally allows. Studies on the "rigid" child show that uncertainty about what he is "supposed" to do, and lack of understanding about why it should or shouldn't be done, encourage many children to play it safe in particular restricting ways. They will push experience into broad categories of "right" and "wrong" and stand stiffly between them, unable to make the slightest adjustment. I met many children who became really upset at a deviation from routine, and who clearly needed the security of repeated familiar behavior. Desperate to "know," they clung to certainties and insisted on constants. I remember one day when Cathy and I were having cocoa in the school classroom how she refused to stir the cup with her finger when I added much-needed sugar. No matter how I assured her it was okay, and that it was my "fault" for forgetting the spoon, she would not and, I saw by her tension, actually could not dip her finger into the beckoning liquid. Mommy didn't like her to stir things with her hands, she told me again and again. But this is "different," I countered each time, not being aware enough in my own frustration that for Cathy there could be no "different." You don't get your fingers dirty, period. It doesn't matter that it's now a cup of cocoa instead of a once dirty diaper, or that there are extenuating circumstances for violating a family rule of manners. To make such a distinction would suggest an individual evaluation of experience that Cathy is too uncertain to make right now.

Dr. Arthur Jersild says that toward the end of childhood a child can "disengage himself from the unpremeditated flow of feeling and thought and examine the flow, question his ideas, inquire into his motives and scrutinize the fabric of his life."

But in childhood itself most children can act only in consonance with conditioned responses and sometimes, like Cathy, must keep these responses well oiled by rigid repetition. Studies on children who are far more rigid than any children in this book illustrate the ultimate effects of spending too long a time obeying without understanding. One fascinating if frightening bit of research was aimed at seeing how children can accept variations in a scheme. A group of eleven-year-olds was asked to classify a collection of objects —items that covered a very broad field, toys to kitchenware to tools. The results showed that children who were considered "rigid" could not classify the items in any other way but their obvious functional relationships. In other words, while the nonrigid child could see the connection between the redness of a toy and the redness of a wrench, the rigid children could not. Toys were in one pile, tools in another, pots in another—and there was no other way of sorting they could think of.

Similarly, when given a series of cartoon pictures which showed a child breaking a rule that was written across the top, they could not qualify the rule's moral judgment. For instance, one picture showed an old woman sprawled on the street, the contents of her shopping bag littered around her. The child in the picture is offering her help, although the written rule says "Don't talk to strangers."

As with Cathy, the rigid children absolutely could not relate to the idea of extenuating circumstances. The old woman must stay right where she was despite her obvious distress. Their own need to avoid the distress of wondering whether they were doing the "right" thing forced them into the kind of unequivocal thinking that left no room for independent reasoning.

But the cognitive bind of childhood doesn't stop with rigid postures and inflexible judgments. For the lack of "knowing" that is part of being a child is in fact a double bind. If children are often unhappy over having to behave in ways they don't understand, they're also frequently anxious because their limited intellectual powers distort what they're trying so hard *to* understand. Half-truth upon rumor upon childish folk tale are strung together into a bit of totally "logical" wisdom that can be terrifying in its subjective truth.

"If you dig too far you'll fall into China; if you swallow a pit a tree will grow in your stomach; when you start kindergarten you're already expected to know how to read. Babies come from seeds and storks and plants; and when you die a witch comes to take you away in the middle of the night; and if a light goes out inside a tunnel when you're driving, it means there's a crack in the wall and all the cars will fill with water and everyone will drown." These are just a few of the awesome absolutes of childhood, often shared in spine-chilling "can you top this one" horror with other small truth-seekers, but rarely communicated to the grownups who might separate fact from fantasy fear.

For the same reasons that children smilingly obey rules that they resent, don't understand, or are unhappy with, they keep much of their misinformation to themselves. They are afraid of criticism, of disapproval, of ridicule, and what's more, they're not being taught to believe that anyone is really interested. As Dr. Jersild says, "a policy of encouraging children to evade rather than face their personal concerns is deeply imbedded in our culture . . ." so that "a wide gulf often exists between a child's most pressing preoccupations" and what he thinks those around him really want to know.

This communication blockage has some really unfortunate implications, not the least of which is that a child frequently hauls around the bulky burden of false and often nightmarish conclusions. Recently Robert served as grisly, but graphic, illustration of what I mean. He had been an observer of the rapid deterioration from cancer of their next-door neighbor and closest family friend. After an almost total wasting away, the man died, just before his thirty-fifth birthday. During the same period, perhaps out of a new consciousness of the calendar, Robert's father put himself on a diet. With the usual tedious self-involvement of the dieter, how much weight he was losing dominated nearly every family conversation.

Robert's father's birthday was in the spring, and as winter melted along with his excess poundage, it became obvious that his son was acting somewhat strangely. Always sensitive, now he was moved to tears by the slightest criticism. Never happy about being separated from his mother, now he had an infinite number of new excuses for not going out to play, and a thousand and one body ailments to justify staying home from school. Added to this was a suddenly voracious appetite. He would gulp down his food at the dinner table and request second helpings while his parents had barely begun eating. And when they stopped eating he would reach over with his fork and grab anything left on their plates.

"Even vegetables, for Christ's sake," his mother says now, remembering (still rather grimly).

Finally it became apparent that there was a message in Robert's behavior. Though he wasn't saying anything with words, he was clearly communicating quite serious distress. Sufficiently upset herself, his mother consulted their pediatrician, who referred them to a child psychologist. It took only two visits to discover that Robert was living with the fear that his father was going to die in April, on his thirty-fifth birthday. With the inescapable "logic" of his own six years, Robert could not escape from what his parents' friend's death, his father's loss of weight and his father's approaching birthday all added up to. The eating binges reflected his anxiety over the terrible emptiness of this dreadful totaling. Acting out the fear it was so hard to express, he tried to fill up the imminent void of his security by a gulping symbolic expression of his feelings.

As soon as he could admit his feelings, could, with the help of the doctor and his parents, put them into words, escape was newly possible. By being brought out into the open, his concerns could be dealt with.

Yet much of childhood continues to be lived in the dark. As Dr. Jersild and others suggest, we do not educate our children either to reveal or to study themselves. At the same time, as this chapter suggests, for a long, long time, even with encouragement, the results of that study for a child will be extremely limited. As a child, he must spend a good part of his time divorced from real understanding. And to live without understanding means he must always walk the precipice. He never really knows where the next pitfall is, whether the turn up ahead is dangerous. Because he doesn't know, he must depend on others for guidance. And his inability to make the trip alone deepens his sense of inadequacy.

What's more, as he walks, grasping tight the other person's hand, bodily and emotional changes buffet him, make him weave from side to side—sometimes giddily, but sometimes in trembling, throbbing pain.

Childhood, then, is process and, as process, a trip through time and personal space that we can only begin to understand from the places we ourselves have arrived at. . . .

We are watching television one afternoon, and a child star is infuriating the handful of children who share my den. He's so "phony," "unreal," "snotty." "He thinks he's so tough" . . . "acts like he's so big." Nancy turns to me in disgust and says, "How can anyone think he's like a real kid?"

Casually I ask, "What is a real kid?" knowing the discrepancy has something to do with the young actor's air of arrogant confidence. We're not trying very hard for clues to childhood today, and so words only dust the room, without anything really getting settled. But then, after a commercial for a favorite candy, Andy says, amused at the thought, "Being a real kid is like being a candy bar. You keep melting in your hands!"

What feelings they hold in their hands, these real, not mythic or media's children, with all their stains and changing shapes, are the stories we will continue telling now. . . .

3 / Fear

"Every day I'm afraid of dying"

"As soon as I found out that my two guinea pigs, Perry and Juanita, were dead I was terribly scared. That morning I had fed and played with both of them. I just ran up to my room and cried. When I was done I told my parents to please get rid of them. I was very very sad as I cleaned out their cage and threw out the food. Now, in drama, when we're asked to think of something scary, that's what I think of. How the next morning when I went downstairs and when I passed the place where their cage was I got very upset and I got an empty feeling . . ."

A while ago, Greta was hospitalized with some minor but necessary surgery. It was not a hospital that allowed parents to stay overnight, and Greta's mother was assured such emotionally protective procedures weren't actually necessary for the "average" child's well-being. The magic word had been said. Who wants a child who's "different"? So she bowed to the hospital rules and left her six-year-old daughter each night to return home to her other children.

The first signs of trouble appeared one morning several

days after the operation when a nurse stopped Mrs. Walters as she came off the elevator. It seemed, Greta's mother was told (with disapproval clearly piercing professional blandness), that Greta was taking toys from the other children in her four-patient hospital room. During the night she would climb out of bed and raid the night tables of her roommates. In the morning, her own table would be piled high with their books and games and candy boxes. Understandably, Greta's roommates were outraged, and "obviously," the nurse said tersely, the hospital could not tolerate such disruptive behavior.

Mumbling that this was very unlike Greta, and feeling as if she'd been struck by some terribly foreign force, Mrs. Walters hurried to her daughter, who was lying with her face to the wall. Hardly the picture of an aggressive predator, she seemed even tinier than usual. Her body looked shrunken, as though some powerful pain were crushing it. Yet Mrs. Walters knew that Greta was free by now of any real physical discomfort.

Conversation between mother and daughter was sparse, with Greta claiming in halting whispers that she was "too tired" to talk. So Mrs. Walters could only sit tensely by her side, silently wondering what was happening. She could understand that Greta might be depressed over being in the hospital, but why to this extent? And what were the roots of her bizarre behavior? By the time the surgeon came around for his daily visit, Mrs. Walters was quite frantic. She gestured with urgent pantomiming that she wanted to speak with him, but the doctor didn't respond to her invitation. Instead he pulled a chair up close to Greta, from whom no invitation at all had come. As with her mother, she maintained a stony silence, answering the doctor's questions with barely audible brevity. The doctor, however, stayed on, taking the little girl's hand in his and stroking it gently while he talked.

"Greta," he said, "I hear you've been piling up a lot of stuff every night on the table here."

The body under its white hospital blanket stiffened, seemed to withdraw even farther from accusatory sight.

But there was no accusation. Only a sharing of information. A kind of "telling" aimed at releasing Greta from her confused and frightened isolation.

"You know, I had a patient here last week," the doctor said. "She was just about your age. She was very worried that while she stayed in the hospital her brothers and sister would take all her toys and books and records. . . ."

He paused, to let the words be heard fully, and then continued. "I told her that lots of times children in hospitals worry about such things. They're even afraid that when they go home or back to school, people will have forgotten them altogether. I told her that this was just a kind of hospital worry, and that people would never forget who she was. . . . And you know what?" he asked then. "She called me yesterday and said her family gave her a big welcome-home party, and that instead of her toys being gone, she had even more than before, because she got so many presents!"

The doctor let his words penetrate the murky veil of Greta's fear, keeping his hand over hers, so she could grasp it. She turned now, the tears flowing freely and visibly down her face. Sadness still covered her like another blanket, but she was no longer hiding under it, and her eyes already seemed less haunted. For, as had happened with Robert's anxiety about his father's dying, the doctor had put into words what Greta, at six, was not able to articulate even to herself. In these early years of her childhood, there were no clearly printed labels to be pasted on her terrors. Ideas like separation anxiety and fear of displacement and lack of control over life are adult vocabulary. But the emotions they describe can flood a child's being, as they flooded Greta every night.

Since to a certain degree the word creates the thought, helping Greta concretize her thoughts by giving her the language to express them began to evaporate her tension. Till now, all she could do was what Robert had done with his compulsive eating—act out her feelings through her behavior. The displacement she felt from her family was, in the absence of words to express it, translated nonverbally into stealing. She was quite simply doing to other people what she was so terribly afraid was being done to her. While her roommates slept she invaded their lives, taking their favorite possessions when they couldn't protect them. And each stealthy grab at a book or toy paralleled what she unconsciously believed was taking place back home behind her defenseless back.

Blessedly, the alert physician was able to interpret the language of Greta's behavior and respond to its anguished cues. In talking about it, Greta was also given the relief of a significant discovery—her apprehension wasn't unique. Other kids in her position felt the same way too. This is no small source of comfort, for children too often see their fears as a contemptible symptom of weakness, to be hidden, above all, from other people's sight. Dr. Arthur Jersild says that in our culture's preoccupation with courage, "a child may be driven to the point where one of his fears is the fear of showing fear." Therefore, he continues, "when a frightened child feels free to express his fright, and is struck by the fact that others also are afraid, at least a small dent has been

made in the vicious chain of fear and blame through which
[he] becomes alienated from others and from himself."

In any case, whether it's because they fear the shame or
ridicule or punishment which admitting their worries might
bring, or because their anxiety is too free-floating to give it
a name, children are frequently locked with their anxiety into
starkly empty rooms, with only nightmarish specters as company. Innumerable studies document the myth-shattering
truth that children have a great many more fears than their
parents ever realize. In one study, for example, of six hundred children between the ages of six and twelve, each child
was questioned about twenty-four different fears and asked
to tell which were the most upsetting. In arriving at the list,
the study's author, Dr. Eve Lazar, carefully eliminated concerns that were already known to trouble most children, as
well as some that, according to other studies, generally both-
ered very few.

The table now contained a broad spectrum of heart-
thumping possibilities, from realistic worries like being late
for school, to semirealistic ones like being an adopted child,
to what would seem completely imaginary anxieties like being attacked by lions, tigers and snakes. It was obvious from
the results that being afraid, even "unrealistically," is a normal part of a real child's childhood. In evidence, some
findings: 80 percent of the children worried about someone
in the family getting ill or having an accident. Almost 75
percent were scared of being attacked by lions, tigers or
snakes. Nearly 73 percent were worried about their house
burning down, while the same percentage were very frightened at the idea of strange people following them. And 70
percent were terribly afraid of being kidnapped. (With the
recent escalation of kidnapping as a way of instant wealth or

political statement, there's reason to believe this statistic would go considerably higher were the question asked again.)

There's no neatly packaged theory to explain why children are so afraid. A variety of explanations contain fear's quaking rationale, but all support our basic premise. It is, for instance, likely that children get caught in anxiety's web because they can't escape awareness of their dependency, a dependency that relentlessly reminds them of their vulnerability and, what's more, tells them that it will not only take someone older and stronger to protect them from harm, it will take someone wiser to *define* the harm. Which is friend, which is enemy? Which path is clear, which is dangerous? Yes, there must also be some understanding of the expanding world's mysteries before a child can learn not to fear them. . . .

Dougie runs screaming into his parents' bed during a thunderstorm while Greta can, if not terribly happily, remain in her own. The few additional years of living she has had have brought enough flashes of lightning through her room so that she knows they really aren't going to strike her. Safe confrontations with experience expand a child's still limited ability to understand the experience, and thus make it less ominous.

But where uncertainty exists, the fear exists. Simplistically, when I began writing with children in this emotion-packed area, I imagined poems about loud noises and stormy turbulence. Instead their stories and poems ran to the other extreme. The silent menace of the unknown, the subtle terror of a deceptive quiet. A clear relationship, then, between the icy mystery of the hidden danger and the blood-chilling throb of fear.

"Fear is nothing," recites Bruce, beginning a collaborative poem:

No foot shuffling
No talking
Like a very dark night when the shutters swing outside
With a creak you feel more than you can hear. . . .

Picking up on his image, Beth, a serious ten-year-old with large hazel eyes and hair the color of butterscotch, writes:

Fear is like a cold night,
When the darkness begins to creep in
And the cup of hot cocoa in your hands is suddenly
Too cool to warm you. . . .

And Susan continues:

Fear is taking a big step in the snow
    but making no footprints. . . .
Fear is winter when you wake in the night
    and the house is very quiet and you have no covers on. . . .

Later, Robert dictates a poem to an older child who sits at the typewriter. Never having heard the morning's contributions, still this is what he says:

Being afraid is like being in a very quiet room.
There's no noise
at all . . .
Like the no-noise of
a too-soft ball
rolling down a dark and empty hall.

The sense of physical and intellectual inadequacy that comes from being so small in a world that looms so large makes a child hostage to a host of fears—that all in some way relate to his overriding worry of becoming separated from the protective clasp of his parents.

The intensity of Greta's fear of abandonment involved the special reality stress of enforced separation. She had exchanged the warmth of her home for a coldly impersonal, often pain-producing place, where physical weakness and isolation made her particularly defenseless.

But a child's meals need not be prepared in institutional kitchens for him to dine on the indigestible food of separation anxiety. . . .

Jason, four years old, very blond, small for his age, with a vocabulary that would ring true for someone many times his age and size, plays house with a friend. It is a game-playing that, like much make-believe, helps express fear's conflicts.

Jason pretends not to hear the other boy's knock on the door. Finally, however, in a high, ostensibly female voice, he answers, "Go away. You don't live here anymore!"

Eric, his friend, now pretend son, excitedly argues that he does so live here, and he *must* be let in. But Jason is adamant. In sweeping pantomime, he holds the door wide and peers out angrily. Eric's cheeks are flushed, his stance defiant. But he's no match for Jason, who glowers a few minutes longer and then slams the door shut, saying in a voice so loud that it threatens to crack, "Get out of here. I don't recognize you. . . . I can't remember who you are."

Eric's face crumples in terror, matched only by the panic Jason himself knows. As director of this drama, he's led them both into the most revolutionary theater. He has experimented with unimaginable danger, depicted life's most grotesque experience—being deserted by your mother.

Even when the desertion isn't conceived of as deliberate, the out-of-sight, out-of-mind idea keeps children apprehensive. They want to grow up but are afraid to leave the protected circle of home. Afraid that if they step out of the circle the sands of time will cover up their footprints.

So, "If I don't see her, will I ever see her again?" is the persistently haunting question of childhood.

It's a question that sends Dougie screeching down the park path looking for his mother, when he has glanced up from his play and seen she is no longer sitting on the bench where he'd left her. His sobs bring her racing from the water fountain where she's gone for a drink, and her distress is obvious when she hears the source of his hysteria. Sympathy for his fright is touched with concern that he is so "irrationally" afraid.

"How can he get so excited about my being gone for just a minute!" she asks.

But when I ask Robert and a group of his friends to think of the scariest thing that ever happened to them and Robert answers, "One time when I was in the department store with my father and we went down the escalator and I looked up and saw I was standing next to the wrong man"—when I ask my question, and he gives his answer, there is mirrored in his friends' faces full understanding of the descent into hell that brief escalator ride had to have been. And I am able to understand newly that to a child, a minute or two is more than enough time to know the fear of abandonment. Any situation in which a child feels unprotected, in which he can't trust himself to manage the challenge, will be a time so filled with fear that no clock or calendar can accurately measure it.

For one thing, the concept of time, like other concepts, is

in development. Dougie's stomach lunges in immediate panic at a moment's lapse in the continuity of his mother's presence, where Robert might continue playing a bit before becoming really alarmed. But even at Robert's age, understanding of time is limited and unsophisticated. There's little more grasp of its clicking-away complexities than of the difference between morning and afternoon, or day and night. And even these distinctions are made primarily in relation to life's activities. Nine o'clock is when you go to school . . . twelve o'clock is when you have lunch . . . half past six is when Daddy comes home.

But what does "today" really mean and why is tomorrow today when it comes, and how come if I'm smaller my birthday comes before Mommy's . . . ? These are questions whose answers are far beyond a growing child's real grasp (even if a parent could come up with answers she herself was satisfied with). Unfortunately, careless if unwitting adult abuses contribute to this confusion and thus to time-related fears. When we call home from an appointment to tell the sitter we'll be late, and assure the small voice who first answers the phone that we'll see him in "just a few minutes," arrival nearly an hour later fertilizes the field of misunderstanding. Distorted perceptions thicken, making waiting alone in the house "just for a minute, for heaven's sake!" while we run next door for a bottle of milk, seem a sentence of solitary confinement that can stretch to terrifyingly endless lengths.

All through childhood, the absence of security-giving voices through the open doors of other rooms allows fear to move in and take possession of the premises. . . .

"I hate it when Mommy drives the sitter home, and stops off at the store," Beth says. Even the memory seems to distress her. "I always hear these terrible noises, like someone's breaking in."

With her mother in the next room, Beth can tune out the creaking pipes and slapping shutters. But when she is alone, and unprotected, they become newly sinister. The fear of strange noises is great in children of all ages. Indeed, to some extent it can become greater as a child grows older. For the baby in his crib has no concept of burglars. If a noise upsets him, it's only because the sudden sound is startling. It's a different story for Beth, who reads and hears stories about rape and murders and robberies, and so knows that despite its emotional security, her house is not physically immune to invasion.

Understanding this, I am prepared for the story she herself writes, again using pretense to face a real fear. It's a fantasy about a girl whose mother "sometimes put a big block of ice in her stomach so no one could ever touch her without freezing to death." This way, Beth wrote, "when the girl had to be by herself, she was cold, but she wasn't scared. Because she knew robbers couldn't hurt her."

After a few adventures from which the heroine emerged icily intact, the story ended in an obviously anxious author's version of the happy ending. "When the girl's mother came home, she gave her daughter a special drink that made the ice all melt, so the girl could be warm and comfortable again."

When the girl's mother came home . . . Once more the ballad of dependency. A ballad whose recurring refrain should remind us that an aspect of vulnerability is to make the people who protect you heroic in size and importance. And this means that it will never be easy to replace the sustenance of their presence.

Considering the fact that just about half of all mothers today work, and one out of three leaves behind a child under six, we're facing a very realistic dilemma. Society's stubborn clinging to the mythic image of home-centered mother, with nothing more on her mind than what to cook for dinner for her mythically happy children, leaves those children without any well-conceived structure of surrogate care. Too often instead they're subject to hit-and-miss arrangements, under the hands of uninterested, inadequately trained, unresponsive people, people whose presence often fans rather than quiets anxiety. . . .

"I don't like the lady who stays with us when Mommy and Daddy go on vacation," Andy says tensely.

Why doesn't he like her?

"Because," he answers after thinking hard for a minute, "because she smiles too much."

Before we smile in return, amused at the childish illogic, step over to Andy's side of the experience. And remember that the hidden danger is particularly terrible to the child trying so very hard to understand life. Andy can't see behind the obvious pretensions of the lady living with him for two weeks. So for Andy, this gushing lady's false face of friendship is very, very frightening, because it is so clearly false, hiding who knows what awful visage underneath?

At ten, Andy can't, as I can, see the benign quality of the woman's posing. He can't, as I can, distinguish between malevolence and remoteness. He only knows that hidden messages are peeking around her smile's upturned corners, so that he does not feel at all the way a smile is supposed to make him feel. And the impreciseness of it all contributes to his fear, for it reminds him yet again that he can't read the book of his experience by himself.

I ask George, then, about his live-in baby-sitter. Tension tightens the marvelously expressive face when he says he doesn't like her. As with Andy, I seek some hard data, more clues to a child's subjective view of human interaction. But again, as with Andy, the grievances are vague. His rejection and distaste are based on this only: "I don't like the way she talks," followed in quick anger by: "and I don't like the way she looks." It is a sweeping summary that goes no further, and I have heard it before and will hear it again from other four- and five-year-olds, who, like George, are too young to reach even Andy's level of specific criticism. There is no real cognitive grasp yet of false smiles and effusive insincerity. But George has clearly sensed the contradictions in the young woman's behavior, and I know he shares with Andy an anxiety-inducing perception. These people in their lives are too uncertain to bring security. Does she really like him or only say she does? If she gets angry, will she go away? If something hurts him, will she *really* help him? These are the inevitable puzzles of childhood, as children try to figure out relationships. These are the half-formed, fear-forming questions in the struggle to feel safe, to know friend from enemy. These are struggles that at four, in moments of particular confusion, become an anxious assessment of the troublesome person. "I don't like the way she talks, and I don't like the way she looks."

It's interesting to note that how a child himself "talks" is often a barometer of his fear. Indeed, considering the limitations of childhood speech, it may be a better gauge of his feelings than anything he actually says. For example, the quality of George's voice went through obvious changes when he shut the door on his baby-sitter, casually off somewhere else in the apartment, and took me back into the center of his room. I was to be happy captive audience to an elaborate commentary on his collection of hats worn at birthday parties and an intriguing bottle of "magic rocks" and the wonders of his much beloved Slinky toy. There were vitality and vibrancy to his voice now, with his tone changing to match what he was saying and doing: high-pitched glee when wearing a certain headdress, earnest resonance when giving "scientific" explanation.

But listening to the language of the voice behind the spoken word sometimes brings other sounds. Some that ring shrill and tense, or dull and flat. It is a kind of communication that often indicates the emotions inside the small speaker are simply too much for him to handle. They may swirl so fiercely in his chest that he can only shout harshly. They may feel as if they're choking him, so his throat closes up and his speech becomes muffled and difficult. Or his feelings may be so totally deadened by fear that his voice comes out in dull monotone, droning on sluggishly and tonelessly.

When Jason, for instance, talks about his nursery school teacher, his voice is suddenly thick, as if something is burning his throat. Which, of course, it is. The hot lava of his fear of a new place and a new person constricts his chest and tongue. As he tells me these stories . . .

"My teacher follows me home." He meets my eyes, daring me, it seems, to contradict him. When I don't, the impassive response seems to spur creativity. Grimly he continues:

"She wants to hit me . . . she waits downstairs in the lobby so she can punch me. . . . Sometimes she pushes me off the slide in the park. . . . She's going to open the lion's cage when we go to the zoo with my class."

The line between fantasy and reality is a wavering one for children Jason's age. And a very wavering one for the frightened child. So when the elevator doors slide open in the lobby of Jason's building and he looks to see what shadows lurk in the darkened corners, or when the gaily painted nursery school doors swing closed behind him, locking him into four hours of contact with a person he distrusts, his sense of menace is shudderingly real.

The line we speak of is, by the way, not only wavering but circular. For research shows a child who is afraid will read maliciousness and even deliberate cruelty into the behavior of adults who are really quite harmless. So if this woman's personality has heightened Jason's sense of insecurity, his insecurity will distort how he interprets what she says and does.

Indeed, it is this off-center perception that creates Jason's final fantasy about her maliciousness—that she plans to release a lion from his cage, the better to attack her four-year-old victim. Irrational as the fear may seem, studies like the one mentioned earlier prove that logic is not the material from which objectivizations of fear are formed. Not just Jason but great numbers of children worry about being pursued and eaten up alive by wildly roaring animals. From the clammy clay of anxiety are sculpted the moving statues who chase helpless children down manicured park paths or peaceful suburban streets. And the fact is that just as adults influence time-related fears, we have also made our contributions to these childish attempts to give terror a shape.

For in truth many "fantasy" fears are related to the way grownups have conceptualized danger. Greta, for example, is frequently very "worried" about her parents when they go out for an evening.

"It's really absurd," her mother says with a laugh that isn't totally amused. "I actually find myself keeping a curfew for her. Who'd have thought I'd give up my mother's control over my social life for a five-year-old's? There I am, partying, dancing, having a terrific time, and I suddenly feel I have to go home, because she might wake up and be 'worried' that we're still not there. God knows what she's worried about!"

Greta, not just God, knows quite well what she's worried about, although she's too embarrassed to confess it. Instead she masks her concern behind a generalized discomfort that frustrates baby-sitters and continues to puzzle her socially frustrated parents. But after all, since Greta has learned to walk and talk, she's been warned about the dangers in the street. The cars that can run over you, the people that you mustn't talk to, the corners turned that can make you hopelessly lost. How can she not feel worried when her parents are out there, unguarded, in great unnamed spaces, to return, in childish time confusion . . . when?

Similarly, any child who has visited a zoo, and seen lions and tigers and snakes loping and slithering in cages, is able, even with his limited perceptual powers, to figure out they're in cages because they're a threat to his safety. It's perfectly reasonable then to focus feelings of helplessness onto their overpowering threat; a set of fears that in their dramatic proportions crystallize the many things he doesn't feel ready to cope with.

Involved also in fears of this kind is growing awareness of the body's frailty; an awareness that ghoulishly feeds into confusion about bodily functions as well as the healing process. The lion's symbolically gnashing teeth can rip holes in this stuff called skin, and break apart this hard stuff called bones, and the whole business can hurt terribly, and maybe make you some kind of freak for the rest of your life.

Anxiety about mutilation and disfigurement is acute in childhood, appearing of course most distinctly at times of particular stress. Before surgery Greta had enormous anxiety about the prospect of anesthesia, an emotional response well documented in any study of hospitalized children. Asleep, who knows what that knife-wielding surgeon may cut off or take out by mistake, or perhaps by punitive intent? Even simple tonsillectomies will focus light on this haunting projection of doom. When Robert, for example, went to have his tonsils out, he objected wildly at having to put on a hospital gown.

"Why do I have to take my pants off if I'm just going to have my tonsils out!" he demanded shrilly. And in his clutching grip on his jeans is the story of crippling terror. When he wakes up, maybe some part of him much more important than his tonsils will be permanently gone.

Judy went into a panic when her stitches from a minor head injury had to be removed. She clung to her mother, burying her head in her bosom with each snip of the surgical scissors, so that she had to be literally pulled back by the pediatrician each time. But to see the full range of her anxiety we would have to know how Judy pictures her body—that, like many children her age, she envisions it as a kind of container; inside, a bunch of organs bunched together, like cookies inside a cookie box. The stitches that held her together were like the cookie box sealed. The stitches opened were like the box open, its contents now able to spill out, to be (surge of panic) emptied completely. And how quintessentially horrible the knowledge of what happens to cookie boxes when they *are* completely empty . . .

For now, Judy could only cling in terror to her mother, trying not to see those little white fragments piling up on the floor, which were to her mother clearly cotton threads but to Judy maybe not, maybe instead parts of her—parts of her that she was particularly anxious about in this time when new challenges presented themselves, like learning to read. In the worry over meeting those challenges, why not wonder whether the threads weren't really pieces of her brain, and so why not wail at the final snips, and the final flutter to the ground, *"Mommy!* Can I still learn how to *read?"*

Judy's awful measure of anxiety grows out of another aspect of childhood fear. An oppressive sense of retribution. The feeling that, as Jason once said, "it's very bad to be mad" makes many children apprehensive about feelings that are actually, in their childhood, inevitable. For the short-circuiting of pleasure that we call socialization cannot help but be frustrating and anger-producing.

No, you can't have candy, stay up late, mess your pants, hit your brother, come with me to the party, be fresh to Grandma. . . . The list is never-ending, the response always unhappy, even if bitterness is kept deeply buried. Many authorities therefore believe a child's fears often symbolize the nagging worry that sooner or later (and he'll never know when) he's going to be punished for rebellious and angry thoughts.

Such fears are often particularly intense when there's a family crisis like the death of someone close. Studies of bereaved children prove conclusively that they frequently feel they are responsible for the tragedy. For instance, Bruce's much loved but senile grandfather spent the last few months of his life in Bruce's house. His sometimes abusive ranting and senseless demands were very upsetting, and many times Bruce muttered under his breath that he wished the old man had never come to live with them, and he wished he would go back to his own house, and yes, on a number of occasions he wished he would "hurry up and die."

How awful that memory when, a few weeks later, Grandfather unexpectedly did die. Almost immediately, Bruce became tremendously fearful. He read danger into experiences he had happily mastered many months before. Going on bike rides with friends or playing with neighborhood animals were suddenly fraught with danger. Like a criminal on the run, Bruce lived in breathless terror. Perceptive probing by his parents helped him deal with reality and rid himself of the fantasized guilt which, as we shall see elsewhere, can create so much pain.

To some extent Bruce's dismay relates to the earlier-mentioned research into childhood fears that showed children are, in addition, extremely afraid of dying and death. Even children much older than those involved in the research prove, in other studies, to be a lot less sure of immortality than they may appear to be. Those cool, somewhat contemptuous adolescents, it turns out, worry a great deal about life coming to an abrupt and too early end. Perhaps at the wheel of the family car they may arrogantly demand to be allowed to use.

Almost 40 percent of teen-age girls, for example, according to one study, are extremely anxious when they're driving, while 47 percent of teen-agers in general, despite long-suffering protestations to parents not to be so "up tight—Billy's a terrific driver!" are rigidly nervous passengers when Billy does the driving.

Yet few parents are aware of this crack in the adolescent's self-confident façade, just as few parents in Dr. Lazar's study knew how much the fear of death darkened their younger child's horizon. One of the more interesting aspects of Dr. Lazar's research was her attempt to discover how aware mothers were of what their children were really afraid of. In every category there were great discrepancies, with mothers invariably ascribing far fewer fears to their children than they really had. The widest discrepancy, however, involved the fear of dying. Only 10 percent of the mothers thought their child ever worried about death, while more than 80 percent of the children in wild-eyed yes-saying immediately admitted to the fear. . . .

Like Jason, Robert and a friend play make-believe.

"Bang, bang, you're dead!" Robert shouts, and his friend cooperatively falls to the floor. Robert looks down at him, cheeks flushed, and then suddenly pulls him to his feet. "I don't want you to be dead that long. Get up . . . get up!"

They go into the kitchen to have a snack, but even as cookies and milk cover up the last few minutes' tension, Robert retains the mind-boggling knowledge that something happens to people that makes them stop being people and, unlike this game, it is not reversible.

That night when Robert goes to sleep he has a nightmare, where a "death man" comes to take him away. And the next morning he asks his mother all kinds of questions about how long members of his family live and whether it hurts to die, and do you talk when you die, and where do you go when you die, until his mother nervously succeeds in changing the subject, if not, however, the direction of Robert's thoughts.

There was no conscious desire in Robert's mother to isolate her son with his fear. It was simply that she, like the mothers in the study, turned away from children's death-related terrors out of frustration, because they didn't know how to answer questions about death in terms comprehensible to a child. Furthermore, we live in a time when there's little cultural glorification of death, and most of us are uncertain about religious beliefs that once gave the end of life meaning. So the questions our children ask remind us of our own brooding inquiries and we would rather not be reminded, thank you.

Also contributing to children's fears, as well as to parents' discomfort in handling them, is the fact that the world we're all part of is an increasingly fearful place to be in. Anger and despair bubble underneath the surface of all our encounters.

Beth and her mother witness a mugging. . . . Robert's father is verbally abused by a stranger in a restaurant parking lot who feels his "space" has been taken. . . . Andy sees a young man having a "bad trip" on the subway. . . .

And how do we explain that in addition to our list of holidays commemorating famous people's birthdays, we now remember the days of their assassinations? And what about the murders, and bombings, and kidnappings, and hijackings that bound into our living rooms with electronic intimacy?

There is clearly a sense of danger in the contemporary air. Yet our awareness of violence makes it even more important to tune in to the fears which that violence engenders in our children. It is not really a parent's job to provide evidence why they shouldn't be afraid. What is needed instead is our acceptance of their right to *be* afraid, lest we help to force a child's fears underground, entrapping him in the loneliness of the mythic childhood, where it can become more and more difficult to feel "safe."

4 / Loneliness

"Feeling lonely is how the street looks
just before it gets dark"

Nancy writes this description of her lonely feelings after her family has gone out for a Sunday walk, leaving her at home to nurse a cold. Her grandmother, here on a visit, is resting in the next room, so Nancy isn't afraid of being alone in the house. Yet she is suddenly overcome with anxiety and a deep feeling of sadness as she sits curled up on the window seat in her bedroom. Outside on the street she sees her father playfully pulling at her sister, and her mother laughing and hugging her brother. The glass that separates Nancy from the happy cluster seems to condemn her to isolation, as the sun shining on the intimate scene outside rapidly fades and darkly colors her vision.

Jeremy is twelve. He is awkwardly tall and much too thin, seeming to be all bony legs and arms. His days are marked by clumsy accidents that frustrate him sometimes to the point of (secret) tears. He is leaning against a tree in the school playground while his class team finishes a game of ball. A little while ago he'd heard the coach insist that he be given a chance to play, and heard, too, the team's grudging acquiescence. When Jeremy, nervous, fumbling, made a mess of his pitching, disgusted shouts followed him from the field. Now, off alone, he feels his eyes smart, and he keeps looking down at his hands as if they still held the baseball, as if he were figuring out just the right curve it would take to strike out an opposing player. With such a victory, he might be accepted by the team and, more importantly, by himself.

Tommy still has nightmares over his bunkmate's drowning at camp last summer. It was Tommy who noticed the boy's absence, and who tried to track down the wet bathing suit that would say Steven had indeed returned from swimming and was just off by himself somewhere, the way he tended to be.

Tommy at fourteen is an immensely capable person. He is stocky and of only average height but extremely well coordinated. The supremely methodical member of a family of disorganized artists, he has always enjoyed the structure of camp life and frequently found Steven's inability to deal with it quite maddening. Steven was, among other noncamp things, a "loner," the child who so often seems apart from the places he is physically part of. Whether Steven's isolation was self-imposed or only meek capitulation to other people's rejection Tommy now, terribly now, will never know. For Steven's bathing suit was not found that afternoon. He was still wearing it when his body was dredged up from the lake several hours later.

The emotional state of the campers that night didn't reflect their earlier attitude toward the dead boy. Tears and shrieks and sobs rolled over and through the gaily cluttered cabins, in one of which, despite the late hour, one bed was glaringly well made. Tommy alone remained stoic, seemed untouched by grief. His mother, who came to visit when she heard the news, was troubled by his apparent lack of feeling. It seemed so strange, because the counselor told her that Tommy was the only person who had ever made Steven any real overtures of friendship. However, it soon became apparent to Tommy's perceptive parents that his remoteness was in fact connected with the tragedy, even if they couldn't figure out exactly how. All that summer and on through fall he retained the thoughtful, quick-to-anger manner that spoke of some desolate inner turmoil.

Tommy and I were friends. We visited often and talked about many things. But he never discussed the drowning until one day just before Christmas when he told me about getting a letter from a girl at camp, who was starting a scholarship in Steven's name. Everyone thought it a fine idea, she said, but it was clear Tommy didn't think so at all. His cheeks were flushed with resentment, and he threw the letter on the ground after reading it to me.

"She's such a phony," he spat out bitterly. "She never would even say hello to him. None of them ever knew he was alive. . . ." And then he showed me a poem he had written, which he was enclosing with his parents' generous contribution to the fund—a chilling addendum to a warm human gesture.

> Steven Hines, not known to all
> Became well known when he went
> and died and
> Left all the girls crying
> Popular now in death
> a damn shame in life
> that I was his only friend
> up there
> The one who didn't cry just
> for the heck of it.

While Tommy believes he did try more than his camp-mates to touch the depths of Steven's loneliness, he is haunted by guilt that he didn't try enough. That evening, over a dinner I shared with his family, it all poured out. The retrospective evidence of how he had so often, too often, turned away from Steven's outstretched hand. The walks he didn't take with him, the games he declined to play with him, the conversations he cut short so quickly. A relentlessly negative bill of particulars that was climaxed by Tommy's harsh whisper to his father—the choked suggestion that maybe there was some terrible connection between Steven's loneliness in life and the fact that his life was now over.

Tommy's parents quieted his disproportionate feeling of responsibility for the other boy's death, but the thought that Steven may have taken his own life is not simply the melodramatic musing of an adolescent. The ugly fact is that suicide is the second major killer of children Tommy's and Steven's age. Only accidents rate higher, and who is to say how many of those accidents are not themselves premeditated decisions? Is the drowning really from a stomach cramp? Is the car crash really the result of inexperienced driving? Is the overdose of drugs only the arrogant refusal of youth to consider consequences?

There is hardly a way to know. But what *is* known, brutally and inescapably, is that more young people than ever before are trying to kill themselves, and equally escalating numbers are being irrevocably "successful." The wish to end life before much of it has begun now affects about eighty thousand young people every year, with data accumulated on children attempting suicide when they are only ten years old. About ten thousand children from ten through adolescence make melancholy intent a final reality, a figure twice what it was fifteen years ago. Proof once more that contemporary stress makes it harder to be a child. On examination, it turns out to be the stress of loneliness that is chiefly responsible for these suicides. The difficulty in communicating, the feeling of separateness, the dreadful sense that your presence is neither needed nor noticed make some children want to cease living at all. Fewer than 30 percent of these boys and girls who kill themselves even leave a farewell note behind. No one to talk to in life, why bother trying one more time, in death?

I am in no way suggesting that every child who feels lonely is or will be suicidal. The despair of the young people responsible for these burgeoning statistics doesn't fall within that range of "normal" feelings we are considering. Their pains are greater than those known by the children who live inside these pages. But once again, behavior seen in its extreme can often make clearer the continuum between "normal" and "abnormal." There's a recognizable truth under the exaggerated act, and it is this truth, the truth of loneliness in childhood, that we pause to look at.

Actually, the experience of loneliness is remarkably elusive. There are so many nuances and degrees, so much variation in its expression, that no one, psychiatrist or poet, really believes he can totally define its slithery shape. Nonetheless, young poets in particular will often try. . . .

Beth writes:

> Loneliness is like an asthma attack
> I feel sick
>   and sick
> it's hard to breathe
> my lungs hurt and hurt
> Happiness goes

> in and out
> in and out. . . .

All the children agreed when Beth read this that there is often real physical pain attached to loneliness. Headaches, stomach aches, muscle cramps and certainly chest constriction can be body signs of a child's battle with its multifaceted terror. And it *is* multifaceted, this exquisitely painful feeling, which is why it is so particularly hard to define. And why, also, it so encircles childhood—making some experience of its isolating presence inevitable.

There is, to begin with, the loneliness that grows out of a growing child's need for love. Children are, we know, born with the need for warmth and tender contact. Quite apart from their dependence on others for physical survival, their sense of worthwhileness and emotional security comes from other people giving and showing love. Experiments prove conclusively that the hand that feeds must also hold and stroke if an infant is to escape emotional and maybe even physical crippling. A study was carried out at Johns Hopkins University among children who were extremely undersized. Their problem was thought to be hormonal, until investigation showed they were all deeply lonely—that they were boys and girls who came from families where tenderness was conspicuously absent. The hospital staff was instructed to show expressions of love along with the standard medical care. Cuddling and caressing and intimate conversation became part of the therapeutic scene. The results were rapid and, as the report reads, "remarkable." There was dramatically noticeable growth in these bodies that had apparently been stunted by emotional isolation.

The loneliness of childhood, as it relates to being taken

care of with or without tenderness, is mirrored in the stories
of these biologically "atypical" children. But the most physically normal "normal" child will also experience loneliness
when he temporarily loses the security he knows through
love. Invariably in descriptions of loneliness, children will
refer to feeling cut off from intimate contact. . . .

Greta dictates, "Being lonely is eating lunch with your
family in a restaurant, and no one talks to you."

An older girl writes wistfully, "When I feel lonely, I
remember when I was a baby and looking for my mother
through the bars of my crib. All of a sudden, it's like here
I am again, in an empty room, still only looking."

And an adolescent's imagery also captures the bleak sense
of estrangement so often felt by the lonely child:

> I try to shake hands
> with my father
> across a fence.
> > But,
> his side is higher
> than mine.

The intense longing for interpersonal intimacy and love
that's part of childhood is heightened by the restricted possibilities of the nuclear family. The lonely feeling of "separateness" feeds into and is fed by fear of separation. Because
this is so, another loneliness-related problem takes shape.
That utterly desolate idea that we deserve our despair (an
idea most adults grapple with for a lifetime) begins in these
early days. As a child tries to understand his pain when he
loses sight of love's face, he can only blame himself for failing
to keep it nearby. Jason, for example, has no capacity yet to

appreciate his mother's artistic talent or understand her need to express it. All he knows is that five days a week the door slams shut behind her and for long stretches of time he is, in spirit, alone. It's quickly obvious, when I talk to him, that at the age of four, two and two put together frequently total self-blame. Something about *him* makes her prefer her studio to being home. If he were better, nicer, she would want to keep him company. The mornings in school with his "mean" teacher, the trips to the park, where so many other kids come with their mothers (not like him with a grumpy nursemaid), are his fault. It's his fault he's lonesome. He is essentially unlovable.

If this seems an extravagant reading of Jason's perceptions, I assure you it's not. While such reasoning does not always dominate his thinking, at various vulnerable moments it will do exactly that. Just as it will for other children Jason's age who are in similar situations. As "magical" center of all experience, with little understanding of the many influences on an event, young children often have only themselves to blame when the magic and resulting event are black.

It's out of this kind of thinking, in fact, that another kind of loneliness comes. The terribly alienated feeling that they must keep parts of themselves guiltily hidden from other people and, to some extent, even from themselves.

Andy writes this poem one morning, his face flushed with anger. The capital letters and their implications are his own.

My brother bothers me. . . .
My mother gets mad at me when I hit him
I never hit him
I never tell on him either
I never tell anyone what he does to bother me

I MIND NOT TELLING
I love my brother.

Andy has been taught it's "wrong" to be seriously angry with his brother and to express that anger physically or verbally. The conflict over what he feels and what he's "supposed" to feel is obvious in his quick assurance that he loves his brother after that instinctive upper-casing of his resentment. But as Andy denies his spontaneous feelings, his isolation deepens. For he gets further and further away from his instinctual self. And a conviction grows, whispers bleakly in his ear, that if people knew what he was really like, they would not, could not, should not love him.

This shame-tinted, isolating secrecy extends to confessing even loneliness itself. There's something not nice about being lonely, including the kind of loneliness that's profound and profoundly justified. Greta, for example, knew in the hospital the loneliness that speaks life's basic truth: Each person stands, in certain moments, alone. For Greta during those two weeks there were many such moments. The fundamental separateness of existence hovered around her as yet limited comprehension; she went, alone, through the terrifying technology of tests; received, helplessly, the smothering mask of anesthesia and was wheeled down corridors on narrow canvas stretchers without the power to stop the process. All children, even if they never set foot in a hospital, will at certain times (away at camp, entering a classroom full of strange faces) catch a glimpse of this solitary side of the human condition. Unable, afraid, to share this vision, they feel their confusion and loneliness deepen.

Rollo May called loneliness the "yawning void," and over and over again children spontaneously use the concept of emptiness in their descriptions of what it feels like to be lonely, once again proving they are much more aware of the complexities of emotions than adults think they are. It's the rare child who doesn't know very early in life that being lonely is a lot more complicated than being physically alone. Witness a potpourri of definitions not found in any dictionary. . . .

"I'm inside a deep dark pit. . . ." "It's a huge opening that sucks me inside. . . ." "The walls are as high as the sky and there's no way to climb out. I have to inch my way up the walls, but I keep slipping. . . ." "There's an invisible tunnel that only I can see. It stretches forever, ahead of me forever. There's no opening in sight. . . ." "There's an empty curving hole in the ground that I sit in all by myself. . . ."

So bottomlessly terrible is this emptiness sometimes that children aren't beyond sharing its space with the most dreadful kinds of creatures. It's as if the ghosts and witches and monsters that haunt sleep and even the waking world are still preferable to being lonely. As Dr. Jersild says sadly, it may "be better to have a corpse for company than to have no companionship at all."

The need for companionship is great in childhood and how the need is filled is very much a part of the story of loneliness. There is a lovely children's book that speaks to this yearning —*Charlotte's Web,* by E. B. White. In it, a pig named Wilbur searches the barnyard desperately for a friend. After he has been rejected over and over again, Charlotte the spider makes the commitment. But there's a lot about Charlotte that troubles Wilbur, and he finally says to himself, "I've got a new friend, all right. But what a gamble friendship is!"

There is (again quite contradictory to the mythical child surrounded by smiling chums) a sharp consciousness in children about the "gamble" aspect of friendship. And a great many will often skip the game rather than chance losing. They'll settle for superficial contacts based mostly on shared activities, but they hold back from the kind of intimacy that really could counteract loneliness. For while a friend is described with wistful regularity as being someone you can "trust," who will "help you" and "be on your side," the real truth is that few boys and girls I talked to felt such a relationship existed in their own lives.

Trying to grow up is hard and it's a competitive struggle that pits one child against another. Each person wrestles with his own need for popularity and acceptance, making it almost impossible really to be open to anyone else. Jules Henry, the anthropologist, writes about children and friends: "The fact that everyone can be chosen or rejected . . . makes for enormous uncertainty in interpersonal relations; it makes for great sensitivity to looks, stares, smiles, and criticism, and originates the endless inner questioning, 'Am I liked?' "

Dr. Henry's observation proves faultlessly on target as I see the results of a story game that has friendship as its theme. The children are to make up stories or poems about a set of pictures. George, when I show him a picture of two boys his age laughing, says, "They're telling a secret. . . . I feel sad. . . . They like each other." And Robert dictates this poem about a picture of a gray bird:

> This is a lonely bird that
> I have heard
> is the loneliest bird in the world.
> It sits all day in
> a rotten way . . .
> that lonely bird with
> no friends.

And Cathy writes this about two girls who have just won a trophy:

> They feel fine
> They feel like a person
> They feel like someone
> They feel like friends.

If friends make you a person, no friends can make you a lonely, invisible nonperson.

"I had a dream," Nancy writes . . .

> No, more a nightmare
> I was in school, and they all didn't know me
> I felt so alone when no one knew me
> I looked in my mirror and I was ugly
> I looked in my mirror and I saw nothing
> I'm ugly, I'm nothing when I'm alone.

The feeling of validation that comes from acceptance by other children, and the deepened loneliness when it does *not* come are greatest for the older child. As adolescence approaches, the child begins to detach himself from the family. To an increasing extent, he must come to terms with himself as an independent person rather than as his parents' child. While this process is inevitable and necessary, it can also be very lonely. . . .

"There were many nights," Tommy's mother remembers unhappily, "when he'd cry out in his sleep from a nightmare about Steven's drowning. I'd wake him up and would just ache to hold him and rock him in my arms. But of course he'd be furious if I did anything like that. So I'd just give him some water, and leave him alone."

Thus the child who is emerging from childhood must look harder than he's perhaps done till now for what Balzac once called a "companion for his fate." This is a period, after all, of particular turbulence, when new yearnings and doubts engulf the body and the mind. To know someone, and preferably many someones, also struggling with the turmoil can be extremely comforting. Even if the intimacy level is really low, with competitiveness dominating the scene, having "friends" still makes the landscape less threatening. The mere fact that he belongs to a group makes the child less lonely, for he is, if nothing else, part *of* a group.

So there is comfort, however small, in numbers. Several lonely young people, struggling with growing up, can lessen the individual experience of loneliness. But what of the boy or girl who stands outside the crowded circle? They, too, have to make identity experiments, separate from and become independent of their mothers and fathers. What if, when they let go of their parents' hands, there's no companion's hand to grasp instead—how do they withstand the buffeting of developmental storms?

And the question goes beyond just losing the comfort of sharing experience. There's a concept in children's friendships called "mutual mirroring," according to which a child of any age can, in effect, see himself through his friend's eyes. He can identify with his friend's behavior and adjust his own to conform to what he wants his friend to perceive. The child who has no friends—what can he do? How does he learn to be part of the world if he never enters into its social give-and-take? His mirroring is not mutual but solitary. The image he sees is always his own, unchanged by anyone else's perspective.

What a desolate idea . . .

But maybe . . . not.

For there is another side to loneliness. A side that recognizes the power of each unique image and is not afraid of the single reflection. Children left alone by contemporaries and often by adults as well are in many ways particularly free to discover themselves. And so they frequently do, in highly creative, exciting ways. It was no coincidence that many of the most sensitive, curious and intellectually aware children I talked with had always spent and still do spend a great deal of time alone. Nor was it a surprise to check this finding against the early lives of people who have made significant contributions to the world, and discover that they, too, in childhood had to do without acceptance by their crowding-together peers. For example, Albert Einstein, when reflecting on his life, said his work grew out of very personal and instinctive drives.

"For the most part," he said, "I do the thing which my own nature drives me to do. . . . It's shameful to earn so much respect and love for it."

"Of course," he added, "arrows of hate have been shot at me too, but they never hit me, because they somehow belong to another world, with which I have no connection whatsoever. I live," he concluded "in that solitude which is painful in youth, but delicious in the years of maturity."

It can be delicious, too, in its way, even *during* youth, the pleasures of self-discovery outweighing the pains of isolation. When I see Robert walking home from school alone, while the other kids group into twos and threes, my heart aches for him. His face is down, and I can't see its expression, and I wonder what he thinks as he walks past pairs and hears shared laughter. But then he bursts through the door and tells his mother he has to call the planetarium "right away," because he has a question his teacher couldn't answer. I hear his discussion with the scientist on the other end of the phone, and the conversation has a legitimacy that seems almost bizarre when Robert hangs up and wets his talked-dry throat with eager gulps of chocolate milk from a dearly loved Yogi Bear drinking cup.

And George, who as an apartment dweller cannot open a front door to a street full of other children but must wait for mother or sitter to take him to the park, has a curiosity about my tape recorder that dominates our interview. How does it work . . . why does it distort his voice . . . can he try it for himself? And he does try it, and in only moments masters it, and there is a delight in his mastery that promises an appreciation of his own uniqueness.

But obviously, of course, even the most well-adjusted child who is most creatively alone will sometimes wish he were not alone. It's at times like these that he may use his creativity for an ultimate invention: giving life to an imaginary companion. Studies show that bright children are particularly likely to invent a fictitious playmate, using its presence to meet very particular needs. For Robert this need is an acceptance of his scientific interest, which so many flesh-and-blood contemporaries find "weird." But to Bo-Bo, Robert's fantasy friend, a "superfish" goldfish, who wears U.S. Keds and Levi's and rides back and forth on a horse, to him Robert's "lectures" on newly learned information are never tedious. No matter how long they last, Bo-Bo's gills never close with drowsy boredom. Greta, on the other hand, uses her imaginary friend, Ming (an orphaned Chinese princess), as a collaborator. Feeling frequently overwhelmed by her brothers' presence, Greta knows Ming is faithfully committed only to her. When the boys dominate conversation, Ming and Greta whisper to each other, often planning intricate plots of aggression that make Greta feel newly powerful.

Greta's relationship with Ming demonstrates that you don't have to be an only child to be in ways a lonely child. Indeed, much of Greta's lonesome sense of separateness relates directly to the fact that there are several children in her family. For there is in childhood an enormous concern with what's "fair," and in the subjective, tentative logic of these years, that evaluation can get quite distorted. So it is that Greta becomes terribly upset when her brothers get bigger slices of cake or more heaping dishes of ice cream than she does. The loneliness of rejection cuts into that smaller piece of cake she's been served, even though realistically it's all she can comfortably eat. Yes, she hears the argument that the boys are bigger and so have larger appetites, but what she feels is a lonely hunger for as much cake (read as much acceptance) as they get. Dr. Jersild explains that children are frequently more preoccupied with the idea of "proportion" than they are with "amount." Therefore, the proportion of loneliness can be quite great for a child who, with other siblings jostling for position, feels she's not getting her fair share of her parents' love.

On the other hand, loneliness has its own particular shape for the child who doesn't share childhood with brothers or sisters. He may indeed use aloneness well, but there are times when it hangs heavy. The lonely feeling that Jeremy described as like "when you're the only person left and you don't know where to run" can be accentuated when there isn't anyone to run alongside. Many only children I talked to clearly preferred the idea, if only at certain select times, of having another child in the family. Andy summed it up for many children when he said he thought "two kids were just right." Why? "Well," he answered seriously, "because one is lonely, and three's a crowd, but two—that's company."

One of the times that company is needed, most children agree, is at meals. Eating alone is an experience that children clearly dislike and that accentuates feelings of loneliness.

This unhappy truth again shows how problems are caused by clinging to a mythic image. Many women's groups are quite properly agitating for provision to be made by school systems so that the child whose mother works can lunch comfortably at school. All across the country there are local ordinances based on some idea of family that makes this impossible. The assumption that children should eat lunch at home makes no provision for children whose mothers cannot be home at lunchtime. And it leaves a child like Beth, through the disapproving dispensation of the principal, sitting on a cold gymnasium bench eating out of a paper bag, along with a scanty number of other lunchtime pariahs.

Living as she does in a quite traditional community, where large families and home-based mothers prevail, Beth, as the only child of a working mother is set apart (as the city child might not be, her life style being more modern than mythic, and her schools recognizing her needs). But for Beth, the solitary lunching intensifies the loneliness of being "different." For this reason, while she frequently enjoys the special pleasures of being an only child, when she sits on the concrete bench at noontime she would welcome being crowded by a brother or sister.

Unfortunately, if eating alone can accentuate loneliness, eating itself can become loneliness's antidote. In the months after her parents' divorce, Susan began putting on weight at an alarming rate, and traces of gargantuan feasts still jar her mother when she comes home from work. When I talk to Susan one day, she is eating potato chips, and hospitably offers me some. After I take some in my hand, she eats her own directly from the family-size bag. A look of tension comes over her face and she reaches for the chips with increasingly staccato movements. The eating is clearly joyless and clearly compulsive, and I know in terrible certainty that she will not be able to check the jerky bag-to-mouth motions until there is nothing left in the greasy cellophane sack but crumbs. Hunger, at least physical hunger, has long ceased to be a factor in the food she currently consumes.

To my surprise she admits this, initiates a conversation about her eating.

"I don't remember the last time I was really hungry," she says in a mixture of defiance and apology. "I know I should go out and play more, but I'm always so tired. So I just come home and watch TV and eat."

She pauses, and then, licking the salt from her fingers, she says, "Anyway, it's nice, when I'm in school, to think about what I can eat when I come home. It makes me feel better about coming home when no one's there."

How many jams and candies and spongy breads and sickly sweet drinks are sold to feed the gnawing emptiness of children hungry for human contact?

As I write about loneliness and its impoverishments, I, a non-animal lover, am newly responsive to puppies and kittens and all the other furry, single-mindedly devoted creatures who fill the lonely spaces of a child's life. Far better than Susan's sucking salt from her fingers, or gulping sandwiches and sundaes, would be a puppy's tongue ecstatically licking her face. . . .

"My favorite possession," Jimmy writes for an assignment, "is not really a possession. It's my dog, Mr. Mouse-face. My parents named him that because they think he's runty. But to me he's beautiful. He's always waiting for me when I come home. He kisses me and slobbers all over me and it's sticky and yukky but everytime he does it, I feel great."

And Beth saved for a big tin of her dog's favorite "cookie," and wrapped it in Valentine paper when the animal came home from the vet's after surgery. Inside the box was this elaborately illustrated poem:

Since you've been gone, I've had
nothing to do
but look at
    the rain and think
about you and sing a lonely song.
I cried in my prayer and I
hoped God would hear.
Now you're back!!!!
I look in your
    corner
and you're there to see.
Oh! your old love-face—it
makes
a brand-new me!

A brand-new me is often perceived by children as being an unlonely me. An apologetic self-consciousness is fostered by adult denial that loneliness can affect one very early in life. Yet even Harry Truman, certainly a more pragmatic than philosophic man, was able to recognize the truth of this experience. He's reported to have always gone out of his way to speak to children because he accepted and understood that "it's a very lonely thing to be a child."

Allowing a child to acknowledge this sometimes painful truth can help him hang on to his inner self, a self he will, because he accepts it, feel freer about revealing to someone else. And in that act of unafraid intimacy will be, of course, loneliness's primary antidote.

5 / Guilt

"I do a lot of bad things"

Freud called guilt "the most important problem in the evolution of culture." At the same time he saw guilt as the means by which a culture survives. With a sense of guilt, people can relate to each other productively. Without it, they would be like the psychopath, who sees all other people only in relation to his own predominant needs—needs that recognize no moral measurement of "right" and "wrong."

We already know that feeling guilty is one of the ways a child becomes a dues-paying member of society. When he does something he's not "supposed" to do, he feels the hot surge of self-blame. Inner critic drowns out inner friend, shrieking accusations, warning of terrible retribution for disobeying a parental "shalt not." Similarly, just anticipating guilt inhibits all kinds of behavior that the instinctual self cries out for. . . .

Greta sits over a dish of ice cream and chocolate sauce that she's eagerly watched me prepare. The moisture in the dish is matched by her salivating—but suddenly there's an enormous problem. She's asked me the time and I've told her it's four-thirty—an hour, it turns out, that's past her mother's permissible snacktime.

Greta's conflict is painful to watch. I have the feeling that suddenly her hand is really not able to pick up the spoon and put it into that creamy luscious mound and bring it, heaping, into her hungrily waiting mouth. In front of my eyes she is becoming leaden, stiff, a robotlike example of the "good" child—good here defined as accepting her mother's value that it's "bad" to eat sweets before dinner.

I feel terrible to have unwittingly created this dilemma. And it's literally a dilemma, for neither solution to Greta's problem will in fact *be* a solution. (Definition of dilemma: "any situation necessitating a choice between unpleasant alternatives"!) If she resists the treat, she'll be more than physically starved. Her repression of self's appetite will cause grave tension; a tension, some would argue, that in itself contains much guilt. For in her righteous stoicism, she will have ignored spontaneous needs, and so, according to this view, will experience the guilt of self-estrangement.

On the other hand, if she surrenders to temptation, her flesh will crawl with apprehension. Guilt has been called "moral anxiety," and I find it a particularly accurate description as I watch Greta anxiously wrestle with the decision to eat or not eat the already melting ice cream. It's a decision I'm helpless to influence. I had, in my own guilt, reached for the dish, brightly assuring her I didn't mind wasting its contents. But her eyes filled with tears of deprivation and I quickly pushed it back in front of her. She stared at it a few moments longer, then grabbed the spoon and began to eat.

She had scaled the mountain, jumped from the highest diving board. The plunge into experience was dramatic. The fear of descent was obvious in the racing movements of her eating. No escaping criminal could hurry so to destroy the evidence and thus evade detection.

At Greta's age, being guilty is primarily involved with

being caught. Her anxiety now, for the most part, centers on whether or not her parents "find out" she has broken their rule. Lawrence Kohlberg, in his studies on moral development, sees this response as part of a process of moral reasoning, a process he divides into three levels: pre-conventional, conventional and post-conventional. Within these levels are six ascending stages in a hierarchy of moral valuing. Each step is a bit more sophisticated than the one before, moving toward a kind of ethical system that bears little resemblance to the simplistic morality of the young child.

To Greta, at the pre-conventional level, "right" is what she can get away with. "Wrong" is getting caught. Consequence is her morality, not principle. Many of the problems children have in early life relate to grownups' difficulty in accepting this piece of pragmatic truth. The six-year-old who cheats on a simple test is coldly condemned by his teacher and suffers scary disapproval from his parents. He, not just what he did, seems to be labeled as "bad." This is a self-perception that causes great pain. And it promises far more unpleasant implications for the future than any to be drawn from his passing off someone else's knowledge as his own. Yet while the child called bad may accept the judgment and carry it with him through the years, actions like cheating at this time of life are in reality no barometer of character or any indicator of future moral development.

Continuing with Kohlberg's widely accepted theory, the next level of moral reasoning is the conventional stage, where, as the name implies, a child assumes the conventions of the family. Now he is prim preacher of their doctrine, not only conforming to the rules himself but "justifying" and "supporting" them to other people. Listen to younger and older children playing and you get a vivid picture of this parrotlike process at work. Senior members of the group dress up in grown-up values in a fancifully imitative game of moral "house."

Jason is playing with a bunch of children in a neighbor's apartment. Uneasy about the relatively unfamiliar territory, but unable to withstand his body need a minute longer, he asks where the bathroom is. Inside, he starts to take down his pants, when he hears the ominous thud of the door closing behind him. Immediately his face reddens with fear and he clumsily hobbles to the door and opens it. Lisa, his friend's ten-year-old sister, primly tells Jason, "We don't leave the door open when we go to the bathroom."

"Yes we do!" Jason yells. He pushes the girl's hand away before it can repeat its assault against his security. His pants are open and falling around his knees. The other children have come near to see the source of the noise. Their giggles reinforce Jason's physical and emotional distress. His penis is now pulsating, his pants slipping from his awkward clutch. He is mortified by his nakedness, and the naked evidence of his fear; and miserably confused by the squirming feeling of guilt brought on by his attempt to satisfy a need for human contact.

Social training has conditioned the older children to recoil at someone's leaving the door open when he uses the toilet. A set of negative emotional responses has created a modifying effect on their behavior. *They* would *never* do anything like *that!* And despite his fear, their disapproval affects Jason, who quickly cleans himself and flushes the toilet, and runs down the hall to his own apartment, something he was not supposed to do. He'd been instructed to wait for his sitter to claim him, but the empty hall and the sitter's scolding were preferable to the other children's guilt-producing disdain. While Jason's mother has already begun to teach the unwelcome lesson of closed doors for private acts, the children's jeering disapproval rapidly reinforces this commandment. You can be sure that Jason will have considerable conflict over leaving bathroom doors open in the future. What's more, if he should inadvertently enter a bathroom that someone else is using, his face will burn with Peeping Tom guilt.

He has learned aversion's lessons well.

Children may move through the stages of moral development at different rates of speed, and at certain times of their lives may be half in one and half in the other. Kohlberg also believes, and observations seem to support him, that people can stop completely at some point in the process. Much work in delinquency, for example, tries to expand and continue the development of moral reasoning so that the "criminal" can really understand why what he's done is called a crime.

Such understanding is best gained in what's referred to as the post-conventional stage. Generally this doesn't occur until young adulthood, although certain of its beginnings can be seen in adolescence. In post-conventional moral reasoning, autonomous valuing takes over. Reason examines shalts and shalt nots, and analyzes absolutes. A distinction now is made between stubbornly upholding cultural mores and developing a set of moral principles, principles that are relativistic rather than based on rigid obedience to any set of rules.

This stage of thinking makes guilt much more complex. We're guilty because of acts against our principles and our fellow man, not simply because of a particular misdeed. So Tommy could feel a lingering sense of guilt over not touching his friend Steven's loneliness while the boy was alive, even though he was in no way involved in his eventual death.

If in this way we can trace the development of morality to see where it takes us, we can also turn backward to see how the guilt attached to this development begins in early childhood. How it flowers in those first days when a child realizes he's a separate person from his parents. In countless ways he starts to understand that his needs often run counter to his parents' wishes. And in that realization is the first planting of the fertile seeds of guilt. For he is bound to do (and to want to do) things his parents won't approve of.

In the process of dealing with this beginning dilemma, he develops what we have come to call a conscience. In psychoanalytic terms it's the superego. To Walt Disney's Pinocchio it was Jiminy Cricket. To a child it's personified in a variety of ways. . . .

"A conscience is something that remembers everything you don't want it to," says Greta in immediate and resigned answer to my question.

"A conscience is an eye in the back of my head under all my hair that sees inside and out," Cathy adds.

Robert thinks for a while, then jumps up and runs to the mirror. He twists his face into a host of shapes, then holds one that's all downward curves and furrowed brows.

"This is what a conscience is," he says excitedly. "A big worried face! It worries about everything I do. It worries about what I say. It's a face that never smiles."

"My conscience," dictates Andy, "sits in a dark room thinking about all my troubles. He's always very, very tired." Andy's voice reflects the same fatigue. His energy seems sapped by the relentless "thinking" of this darkly brooding thing inside him.

The conscience, then, sits in judgment, just as the parent does. Indeed, its authority is often much more heavy-handed than a parent's would really be. Without the intellectual capacity to distinguish between her "sins," a child can torment herself over even the tiniest transgression. . . .

"I broke the plate!" Judy howls the minute her mother enters the door. Her face is taut with worry. All afternoon she'd tried to figure out how to hide the incriminating pieces of glass that shone inside the kitchen wastebasket, so glaringly corroborating her guilt.

Earlier, in bed for a nap that of course wouldn't come, Judy had an idea. She'd dressed and run into the kitchen and climbed on top of the wastebasket, her bottom dipping inside it, her legs awkwardly hanging over the side. It was very uncomfortable, but no matter. When she sat this way you couldn't see the fragments.

For over an hour she sat there, with no TV set to look at, with no one to talk to. Just sitting there. Ready to go on sitting there for how long?

After a while, however, the sitter woke from her own nap, and when she came into the kitchen she burst into laughter at the sight of Judy on top of and half inside the wastebasket. Judy's fair skin went quickly red, her eyes turned to the wall. Shame, the frequent companion of guilt, was along for the ride.

Even when the sitter tried to make things better, pretended not to find her behavior as "silly" as she'd already called it, even when she said Judy's mother wouldn't be upset over a "cheap dessert plate," guilt in all its pain remained. As we have said, a child doesn't distinguish between ideas like expensive and cheap. (Judy still believes five pennies is a much better present than just one quarter.) So what matters to her is not that the plate was made of glass instead of crystal. What matters only is that she, Judy, broke it. That she, Judy, is "bad." And only Judy's mother's repeated assurance that she isn't angry, that she still loves her, that she knows she's really "sorry" can quiet the nagging, frightening voice of self-blame.

At Judy's age, she finds it perfectly conceivable that her misdeeds might result in horrible consequences. She can, this child who has never been spanked, anticipate torturous punishment or that her parents will totally reject her, maybe even throw her out of their lives completely. This bizarrely exaggerated vision of retribution rests with what we know is children's sense of inadequacy, the unhappy feeling that they don't handle things well on their own. . . .

Andy tells this story one morning:

"A boy gave me two chameleons to keep for him when he went to camp, and one died right away, and I didn't want to tell him. And then we went to see my Grandma, and I forgot to leave food, and the other one starved. I felt really bad because the boy was angry at me, but I felt worse for the chameleons because they didn't have a chance."

Beth stands up stiffly and requests a turn as soon as Andy finishes speaking. He starts when she jumps to her feet, as if he expects her to hit him. But she's on a guilt trip of her own. In brittle voice, she tells how she washed her best sweater, her newest sweater, and shrunk it beyond any possible use.

Andy looks up, to share a hurtful moment:

"Did your mother spank you?"

Beth tells him grimly that her mother never spanks her, but that she'd told Beth "lots and lots and lots of times it was a *stupid* thing to do." Her voice comes down hard on the word "stupid." It resounds in the room like a slap, and I realize again that there are ways and ways to inflict guilt bruises on a child inadvertently. And if I needed proof, Beth gives it to me later, when she writes, and reads aloud, this poem:

> It's TERRIBLE!
> It's terrible.
> I can't read
> I can't write
> It's terrible
> I never learned
> I'm not bright.
> Can't you see—it's like
> I'm blind
> I can't do anything right
> I'm poor
> No one needs my poor dumb blindness
> Oh, it's terrible!

What's terrible really is that the most perfectly obedient, well-behaved children with parents who truly delight in them still can't entirely escape guilt's grasp. For there are certain guilt feelings that stem simply from desires, whether or not they turn into deeds. We need only focus on a child's battle with his sexual feelings to see this process. By the time he reaches Jason's age, for example, he's already very aware that certain parts of his body are, in relation to others, a lot more interesting. But even with such permissive parents as Jason happens to have, no child will escape being affected by our cultural taboos against sexual curiosity. That terrific feeling that comes when Robert strokes his penis, or when Judy fingers her vagina, stops when the baby-sitter gives a funny look or the teacher sharply instructs one to sit up straight. In its place they are suddenly self-conscious, uneasy in the sense that somehow, no matter how good it feels, they're doing something "wrong." Faced with the perception that such feelings aren't nice, the pleasure the feelings bring is diluted by guilt. Similarly, Tommy's fantasy over what a female classmate looks like without her clothes on makes him gulp as guiltily when she turns to him as if he'd been caught in the act of disrobing her. And even when sex isn't part of the conflict, the wish to break a rule makes the wisher a frightened sinner. So it is that the desire to cheat on an important test makes Nancy, now old enough to understand the stigma of cheating, flush with guilt when the teacher calls her name, even though her eyes have never left her own desk.

Since it *is* so inevitable for children to feel guilty, it behooves us to examine the many ways guilt may manifest itself in a child's life. For it does, chameleonlike, take on many, sometimes ingeniously disguised, forms. Nightmares, for example, along with a nightmarish number of daytime fears, are often the creations of a punishing conscience. But guilt can harass the body as well as the mind, and so it is often the churning of guilt that produces the painful stomach ache. It is, understandably, hard to digest even the most coveted food when a guilty conscience sits through the meal. And it's equally hard to breathe easily when worry about being "caught" constricts your throat. So the rasping attack of asthma, more often than realized, may have been triggered by guilt.

Oppressive feelings of guilt can even affect a child's posture, his stooping shoulders graphically illustrating a self-punishing weight too hard to bear. In the same way, sudden speech problems may result from losing the battle with guilt. Psychiatrist Sanford Rado explains that, without understanding why, the stammerer "gets scared." There is the nervous feeling that self-expression may bring discovery for secret sins, that what this disobedient, unworthy person says may be (deservedly) held against him. So, says Dr. Rado, "Guilty fear promptly stops his speech, as if to say 'watch your step.' "

However it manifests itself, secret feelings of resentment toward no-saying parents are at the heart of much early guilt. (And as we have already seen, every parent at some point must be a no-sayer.) The range of what's permitted may be greater in some families than in others, but it's a space that has some eventual limits. At some point the gate slams shut, and then anger blossoms. The hostility a child feels mixes badly with his love for and need of his parents. What seem totally imcompatible feelings head toward each other and crash in the harsh dissonance of guilt.

As I've indicated, children are frequently harsh judges of their own crimes. Beth's poem certainly showed that her self-contempt was greater than her mother's annoyance could ever be. I was therefore very conscious when she read her poem aloud that there was at least some element of wanting to punish herself in this declaration of her "stupidity" to her classmates. The self-punitive aspects of guilt are, sadly, nearly always present, affecting, as a result, nearly every aspect of the developing life.

Problems with school, for instance, can frequently be traced to a need to do penance for some infraction or rebellious feeling. When Susan's parents were divorcing, her schoolwork suffered markedly. Her mother assumed her powers of concentration were affected by the tensions at home. She was only partially right, for there was a more subtle slope to this academic decline. In counseling, it was quickly evident that Susan was tormented by the extent of her anger about her parents breaking up. She was also caught in that terrible paradox of childhood perception—helpless to stop disaster, responsible for disaster. So she was guilty, miserably, impotently guilty, thanks to the feeling that it was somehow her fault the family was crumbling. The solution? Punish herself. The sentence? Fail in school. Helping Susan understand that her hostility wasn't unique and that she had a right to feel it and, too, that she had no part in her parents' interpersonal problems broke the cycle of failure. But failure of some kind, in relationships, in school, is a recognized, if demonically destructive way of trying to soothe the wrath of one's conscience through self-punishment.

Guilt can also put brakes on normal feelings of competition and aggressiveness. When I watch Jeremy play ball with seventh-grade classmates, I find myself wondering whether he is not, in effect, "throwing the game." I feel some unconscious bagman has bought him off and that he's making no real effort to win. I am told when I discuss this with psychiatrists that a great many children do indeed slow down inside competition's circle when, out of self-punishment, they can't allow themselves the joy of victory. Reprehensible sinners, they must silently refuse such undeserved rewards as winning games or the approval of their peers.

But at least Jeremy does play, however slowed his pace. Robert at this point in his life won't engage in any competitive sport. The burden of guilt would be too great for him if the team he was part of should lose. Children never have trouble finding evidence in the case against themselves. Robert, at a bumpy stage of development, intuitively stays away from situations that might provide him with additional justification for self-blame. This pulling back from experience out of a fear of being responsible for failure is a bit of footwork most children will engage in at various points in their lives. They generally need help in understanding that they don't have to live up to particular expectations in order to be worthwhile. But in as competitive a society as ours, this isn't an easy perception. Hence the nagging feeling that they've "disappointed" their parents by not getting the lead in the play, or made their friends angry because their poor playing "ruined" the game. Better then, perhaps, not to try out at all for a part or a place on the team.

It should come as no surprise by now that there's an interestingly new wrinkle on the face of contemporary guilt. A great many parents are amazed at the idea that their child should be troubled by guilt. As they react to the idea that their children are fearful, parents recoil from the thought that their child feels guilty.

"Why, I bend over backward *not* to make him feel that way," Bruce's father says unhappily, echoing in his frustration the voices of many other men and women, people who didn't want to "lay that goddamn guilt trip I hated so much on my own kid!" The more I talked to parents, the more I realized that in this time of sophisticatedly antiseptic environments, of polio vaccines and fluoride treatments, we earnestly, if naïvely, try to inoculate a child's spirit against the contaminating germ of guilt. Not to govern through guilt is such an important parental goal, it's a very harsh irony to discover that in spite of it their children frequently do feel guilty. But an even greater irony is that the goal may itself be unnatural, actually creating more problems than it eliminates.

When I visited Dougie's mother one afternoon, for example, he interrupted our conversation with the relentless regularity of a metronome. Each intrusion was a little louder and a little longer than the one she had just smilingly dealt with. There was an air of desperation to Dougie's interruptions, which only seemed to lift when his mother finally put an end to them. Her gentle but firm command that he play by himself until we were done talking calmed rather than aggravated his querulous mood. As if—could it be?—he was looking for some limits to be set, for that line to be drawn soon between permissible and *verboten* behavior.

Yes, it *can* be. For professional opinion confirms what Dougie's mother instinctively knew; that the other side of freedom is often chaos. When all restrictions lift, leaving unlimited space, impulses and feelings can't be rooted or placed in perspective. So while excessive pronouncements of "right" and "wrong" may make children feel excessively guilty, no standards at all can increase rather than diminish discomfort. What *is* right? What *is* wrong? Not knowing makes every action a possible mistake, and makes the limitless space too wide open to feel safe in.

And when they *do* commit a "wrong," children clearly prefer to be punished clearly. Many parents, in the name of liberal parenting, hold back on what seems too authoritarian a response to transgression. Yet there was absolutely no question that the vast percentage of children I talked to preferred direct methods of punishment to the kind of subliminal disapproval their parents indulged in.

"My mother gets this funny look on her face," Susan says. "She looks like a prune, all scrunched up . . ." and she tightens her own face into rigid wrinkles to demonstrate the dry shape of her mother's rejection.

"My father doesn't talk when he's mad at me," says Bruce. "He just says yes and no and makes believe he doesn't hear me when I ask him something. Sometimes it lasts for days.

I can never tell"—he sighs wearily—"how long it's going to take to be over."

Robert has been listening to this discussion of moodily amorphous discipline, and now he interrupts.

"Boy, when my mother gets mad, she yells her head off!" His voice is amused and almost gay, and yes, I see the envy on the faces of our group.

It's interesting to note that punishment itself, not just openly stated disapproval, is also frequently welcomed as a way of wrapping up guilt so it can be disposed of. Jules Henry writes that it may be startling for people in a "permissive culture" to realize that not to be given the emotional pain of punishment can actually "be felt as a deprivation." Yet, says Dr. Henry, "many children would far prefer punishment, for their guilt unpunished becomes emotionally far more painful."

Of course, the punishment must be appropriate and above all fair. No discussion of childhood guilt can leave out the dominant idea of fairness. If guilt thrives on secret resentment, resentment is enormously stirred by a child's eagle-eyed analysis of how just his parents' impositions are. From a remarkably early age, the difference inherent in "do as I say, not as I do" is a difference perceived, and often deeply angering. In one study of children's concepts of authority and rules, it was found they made a clear distinction between rules and fair rules. Invariably the measurement of "fair" was made by how standard it was across all kinds of lines, that it wasn't more restrictive for children than it was for adults.

Children learn morality. As in the case of speaking and walking, they begin to do what they have observed other people doing. But we don't sneakily walk on all fours after we model an upright position for our children. Nor are speech patterns, except maybe for some discreet censoring, very different in or outside a child's earshot. On the other hand, there are often very different definitions of right and wrong for the big and little participants in life's morality play, a difference children are deeply aware of. So while fear and dependence may make them obey a commandment, they are not thereby convinced that justice is being done. Similarly, not even genuine love for their parents will make children blind to the way justice is sometimes bent to fit an adult's temporary requirements. . . .

A few days after Beth had ruined her sweater she came to our class visibly troubled.

She told us that her mother had taken the controversial garment back to the store she'd bought it from, claiming it had shrunk on the very first hand-washing. In fact, it had withstood several washings, and only when Beth plunged it into very hot water in the washing machine was the damage done.

"My mother says they should have warned her it was delicate," Beth says, her voice carrying a tone almost of pleading, as if she wanted someone to reassure her that what her mother said and, more importantly, what she did was right and did not merit the criticism Beth was guiltily feeling.

It was a reassurance not to come from this group. They'd walked this way too frequently themselves. As happened with us at other times, Beth's stories opened up the floodgate of their experience of preaching versus practicing.

"My mother talks on the phone for hours, but I can only stay on for three minutes. . . ."

"My father walks our dog when my neighbor's away so it can go on their lawn. . . ."

"My mother tells her office she's sick when she goes to a party the night before. . . ."

"My mother promises things she says later she didn't mean," Greta announces loudly. "Like letting me cook dinner sometimes, or use the sewing machine. She says she doesn't remember saying I could, but I *know* she said them!"

Her voice rises on the shrill note of guilty rebellion. The class is properly horrified. Breaking a promise, to a child, is an almost immeasurable sin. And indeed, Greta's mother would agree with their perception. Except that the generational difference in assessment of experience makes Mrs. Walters comfortable about her lapse of memory, for she knows she would never break an "important" promise. But —need I even say it?—who is measuring "important"?

Not Greta, that seems certain; whose resentful conflict is unmistakable. Because of childhood's difficulty in freely expressing feelings, she turns her angry feelings inward to fester, and build up, and become distorted. Unable to direct her hurt and anger appropriately, she begins to feel guilty about being hurt and angry.

Perhaps because guilt seems one of the *most* bottled up of children's feelings, they frequently select it from lists of feelings to write about. Because they do, I am able once more to leave the final statement of another childhood experience to those who experience it firsthand. . . .

"Guilt," writes Nancy,

> is like a terrible mess
> A messy rag
> A mess of dirt
> An overflowing garbage can
> that has only my garbage.

And Cathy draws a picture of a big luminous ball and labels it GUILT, and says, "Guilt has a color. It's clear. It makes me feel still and sleepy and think a lot. It makes my house a house no one lives in even when everyone is there."

Robert, too, draws a picture. Of a boy and his shadow. And in perhaps the ultimate statement of guilt and conscience, he dictates:

> This is my shadow.
> He always sees what I do.
> Sometimes my shadow walks behind me
> Sometimes my shadow walks in front of me
> Sometimes when I'm bad my shadow
> punches me
> —because he hates me.

Fortunately, most of the time Robert can believe his shadow finds him fit to live with. But much of the time, nonetheless, the shadowy forms of guilt will hover over his and every child's continuing struggle with impulse and restraint.

6 / Anger

*"Anger turns you into a blackboard
that everybody scratches on"*

Dougie is playing in the park sandbox. A little girl at the
other end makes her way toward him. She stares down at
Dougie, who does his best to ignore her. (He knows too well
what's brought her here.) She's got her eye on his pail and
shovel—toys that benevolently, but in far too limited numbers, are supplied by park fathers. The drama unfolds. Girl
reaches down and grabs. Dougie jumps up and swings. Com-
peted-for shovel now convenient weapon, the better to express Dougie's hostility toward this intruder. Her screams
are piercing as a trickle of blood appears on her forehead. But
they seem only to whet the avenger's appetite for violence.
He comes at her with the pail, dumping its sand mixed with
water over her head. Globs of gritty muck cake her face,
sting her eyes as she frantically rubs them, make blood-
tinged trails of mud down her cheeks.

The screaming victim's mother is horrified, but the trium-
phant villain's mother is no less so. For if we are inclined to
cover up the reality of a child's emotional life, we pull the
covers particularly tight over the feeling of anger. Yes, we
might, however reluctantly, abandon the myth of child-

hood's contentment in order to soothe a boy or girl who's afraid, or reach out to one who is lonely. But there's something so . . . unattractive about the child who's angry, who, like Dougie, blatantly shows his animosity toward another person, or, like Nancy, will whirl ferociously in the blazing center of a temper tantrum. Nancy's furious kicks at the family garden when she's frustrated over some restraint frighten her mother because they seem such an extreme statement of rage. We are a culture that is afraid of the darker side of man's nature. We prefer not to recognize its presence, in others and in ourselves. And certainly we don't want to see it or hear its strident sounds in our children. The fear of what an angry child implies about us as parents, or suggests about how he really, not mythically, sees his world, makes us wash his mouth of the bubbling expressions of bitterness before they're articulated in any direct or indirect way. Dr. Arthur Jersild comments wryly that, indeed, we seem to raise our children in an atmosphere that makes anger immoral, as if, he says, "the eleventh and greatest commandment were, 'Thou shalt not show anger' . . . nor even feel it!"

Yet if we often seem to make little sense in our approach to children, our rejection of the anger they feel is particularly lacking in logic. For the fact is that unpleasant as its scowling face may be, anger is a necessary human characteristic. It is one of the most important ways children can define themselves as people. In anger a child begins to answer life's basic question, "Who am I?" by relating the query to self-assertion. The demands he makes, the rights he defends, his resistance to people who frustrate or hurt him are shaped by the sharp edge of anger. Like a child who is afraid, an angry child is finding a way to cope with an oppressive situation. Dougie, as well as his sandbox adversary, could, after all, have dealt with confrontation by fearfully running to their mothers instead of belligerently heading toward each other. By this measure, then, their defiantly polarized positions were positions of strength which expanded instead of restricted their developing experience.

Dougie and his companion will of course gradually learn to be more civilized in handling their discontents, but their capacity for anger will be an important factor in the people they become. Indeed, one of their greatest "becoming" challenges, as it is with all children, will be how to handle their anger in ways that are strengthening rather than destructive. Learning what aggressive behavior is appropriate and what is not, learning how to mute impulsive rushes of rage, learning what evidences of anger will be tolerated by the grownups in charge and which will be punished are all issues that take up a great deal of a child's time as he tries to figure out what his life is about.

Like many other experiences of childhood, anger to a large degree begins at the very beginning, with a physical response from the infant in his crib. The hungry baby screams to be fed. His clenched fists, his perspiring face and his piercing yell can easily be called anger. But his feelings are unfocused. No enemy has been sighted yet. By the time this baby reaches George's age of four, it will be a tensely different story. A particular person will cause frustration, and so the wish to strike out now takes on a direction.

For example, when I went to see George one afternoon he quickly designed a pattern for our visit. We would simulate host and guest, companionably watch the afternoon fade while we sipped tea together. His baby-sitter had offered to bring me tea, and George told her he would like a cup too. (At four, the kitchen stove is off limits, so he can't on his own implement his design.) While we wait, he takes little bites from the huge gingerbread cookie I've brought as evidence of friendship. To my own need-to-be-accepted pleasure, he breaks off a piece of the cookie and gives it to me, suggests I "save" it to eat with the tea, just as he's going to save the rest of his. Anticipatory delight has given him the ability to delay gratification, but still he impatiently checks the door of his room to see if the young woman is coming. Finally she does appear in the hallway, and George happily stands back to let her enter with the tray that carries only one cup, meant, unmistakably, for me.

There is a rush of expression across George's face as she lightly brushes over "forgetting" his request. Frustration and resentment vie for dominance as they head in her direction. The feelings combine and, in their joining, define the inevitability of anger in a still helpless child's life.

Dependency makes children unhappily accept not only such restraints to pleasure, but also other people's perceptions of their behavior. The labels grownups attach to children infuriate them, since they feel so incapable of tossing them off. Anger smolders silently as boys and girls are given a sweeping summation of their flaws.

"She thinks she's the big boss of words!" George says when the sitter leaves the room after telling him not to be "a baby." While Andy, on another day fresh from being publicly labeled "a slob" by his teacher, grumbles bitterly, "My teacher's a pencil and she writes all over me."

A related and widely held theory about anger in children sees the emotion as growing out of hurt feelings. The loss of face and status darkens childhood with impotent rage and frequently results in grotesque fantasies of "getting even."

Jason and Eric talk about an older child who's been making fun of them on the nursery school bus.

JASON: "I'm going to cut off all his hair and glue it on his nose so he can't breathe."

ERIC: "I'm going to make him drink four bottles of milk without stopping so he throws up all over the floor."

JASON: "Then let's tie him up on the roof of the bus with no clothes on . . . and then . . ."

Now Jason whoops with delight as he gets back not only at the bully but at the restrictive limits of acceptable language. ". . . and then all the birds will make poo-poo on him, and we'll cover him around and around with toilet paper, and he'll be all sticky and dirty smelly!"

Minutes later Jason and Eric are singing a TV commercial jingle. Their rage has passed like a sudden storm. In these preschool years particularly, passion runs fast and high. Had Jason and Eric been strong enough during their flash of anger, they would gladly have killed the taunting classmate, without wasting one thought on the act's morality. On the other hand, the boy himself could soon become a welcome friend should he decide for some reason to be more congenial. Hatred and friendship are equally unstable in childhood, slipping into ever changing shapes while the calendar flips its pages. But clearly, as time moves along its continuum, anger toward someone or at some interference will make young minds and bodies smolder in raging discomfort. This truth of childhood is immediately obvious in the infinite number of references children make to anger's physical aspects. . . .

"When I'm angry," Cathy writes, "I feel like a rotten apple with worms crawling all around me, eating pieces of my insides." And Tommy expresses the rather bleak thinking of adolescence when he creates this terse image: "My body is brittle when I get angry. Like a brick that's used to hole up a fireplace. When you pick the brick up it burns your fingers and then it breaks into pieces."

On the other hand, Robert, at six, is sweepingly dramatic in his descriptions. He colors a piece of drawing paper with huge Magic Marker letters that say "BLIP-BLOP-BOOM!!!!!!" Then, writing skills exhausted, he explains, "Being angry is like being punched in the stomach with a monster's fist." And Lisa, obviously influenced by the day's muggy weather, says, "Feeling angry is like having to drink a big cup of pollution."

As suggested, anger can tear at the mind as well as the body in its jagged ripping of contentment, an experience often perceived as completely enervating. . . .

"To me," Beth writes, "anger is feeling like you're nothing at all. It's when you don't care about anything or anyone." Jeremy shares this alienating vision, writing:

> Anger makes nighttime come,
>   even though it's day,
> You feel trapped,
>   even though you're
>   free.
> You're absent,
>   even though you're
>   there.

One of the reasons anger marks children "absent" is that they rarely feel free to reveal its blistering presence. Although the most important antidote to the toxicity of anger is action, a direct and immediate and appropriately directed expression of the feeling before it festers, children are not generally permitted such release.

In the powerlessness of childhood, they cannot alter the

experiences that fan their anger. Instead, in their helplessness, anger will only grow.

Hear then this tale of impotent rage. . . .

Last month on vacation we went to see a movie in New York. The movie started at 12:30 and we all woke up about 10:00. My brother and me begged our parents to go early so we'd be sure to get in and get good seats. We were all ready to go at 10:30 but my folks kept telling us to do things . . . that we couldn't go until we did them. I got a real bad stomach ache from being so angry at them . . . (we didn't miss it, but it wasn't a good day anyway because I was so nervous and mad before we got there).

Largely because they don't always feel free to reveal anger to adults, children often exhibit a startling Jekyl-and-Hyde demeanor in their daily life. It quickly becomes clear when you spend any length of time observing children that they are often very different people from those they usually let grown-ups see.

Teachers have been known to reel in horror at seeing films of "prize" students theoretically left to their own devices. The quiet, placidly studious pupil who never speaks without raising her hand is suddenly raucously silly and abusively rude to her classmates. Countless schoolrooms, islands of cooperative order when authority is there, become frenzied competitive jungles when the teacher isn't sitting in judgment. Each child stands poised to ostracize, exclude, separate into ins and outs, lightning quick to locate the sore spot in another personality and relentlessly press on it in "better you than me" glee.

One reason schools provide particularly fertile ground for

both feeding and trying to hide hostility is that, for the most part, they make a child ashamed and frightened of his anger. The judgment appears to be handed down that it's not only bad to act angry but, as Dr. Jersild suggests, it's almost as bad to feel angry. Numerous studies show that children fuse and confuse wrathful feeling with aggressive action and see "having a temper" as a very serious defect, to be hidden and disguised as much as possible. Like a pimply face or obese body, it is something to be ashamed of.

Similarly, many children make apologetic analogies between possessing a temper and what it must be like to be "possessed" by evil spirits. Susan, for instance, describes her temper like this:

> It wants this . . . it wants that. . . .
> There is nothing
> that it doesn't want. . . .
> When I try to go away
>   it always makes me
>   stay
>   and hear
> all those awful things it whispers
>   deep inside my ear.

When a child himself can whisper that he does in fact feel angry, there is not only relief, but often a cessation of unproductive yet uncontrollable expressions of his hostility. Harry Stack Sullivan once said that it's a great deal easier to "swallow anger than to digest it," and the fact is that anger swallowed only stores up inside, until finally, often at a trivial provocation, it erupts. One study had as its goal reducing "inappropriate aggressive behavior" in third-grade classrooms. With a study group of 106 children, attempts were made to have them understand the source and accept the legitimacy of their angry feelings. The hoped-for goal was that by "digesting" their hostility in this way they would be able to modify its expression. And indeed, when they did achieve self-awareness in regard to their anger, they were able to apply behavioral brakes to disruptive expressions of it.

This study notwithstanding, schools continue to cultivate a child's indignation by reducing his sense of individuality, as well as his sense of personal freedom. The school as "jail," the feeling of being "locked up" or like "an animal in a cage," appears again and again in children's descriptions of the place they are obliged to go to every weekday (days whose emotional tone Andy described as "giving the Monday morning blahs all the way till Friday").

Andy smiled when he made that comment, but he did not smile when he recited this poem, written after his teacher had "unfairly" included him in a punishment resulting from another student's disruptive behavior:

> I am stuck inside my teacher's desk
> She keeps me inside it
> I keep saying
> LET ME OUT
>   LET ME OUT
>   I keep kicking
>   at the drawer
> One day I'll get it open
> and then
> All she'll have inside it
>   will be

A picture—
that never even looked like me.

Like Andy, many children are often enraged at the loss of emotional and physical integrity that takes place inside school doors. That they must, for example, be given "permission" to go to the water fountain when they're thirsty, or first convince a teacher they're not "faking" before they can seek the nurse's help for a stomach ache, fills the heart to bursting with bitterness. And the ultimate outrage is having to ask permission to go to the bathroom. That someone else has control over their own bodily needs intensifies the futile anger of dependency. Because the level of fury is so great, teachers as permission givers can become the objects of the most passionate hostility unless they have moved into new perceptions of their role and of children's rights. Absolutely nothing spurs a child to faster and fiercer creativity than asking him to fill in sentences that begin, "My teacher . . ."

Jimmy, for instance, begins a go-around one morning by saying, "My teacher is a dangerous weapon because her mouth always punches me. . . ." Robert picks up on this image, seeing, as many children do, the teacher's "mouth" as a major weapon in the school's bruising emotional assaults.

"My teacher," he says, "is a train. Her mouth gives off hot steam that makes you choke if she comes too close. . . ." But it's Cathy who is moved to newly expressive heights by this assignment. She stands stiffly in the middle of our circle. Her voice quivers with feeling as she spontaneously creates this poem:

Teachers are made of sour dough
 a broken toe
 dirty clothes
  and
 a broken nose . . .
 out of mud and grime (especially *mine*).
Teachers have a spider on top
 of their ugly hair mop.
A teacher's job
 is to say no, and
  go
  to the office . . .
and you're BAD—because you forgot your spelling
         book.
I'd like to catch one on a fishing
      hook,
and slit her down the middle
after I washed off all her hate.
Then I'd stick her on a griddle, preheated to
 a thousand and
   eight.
I'd bake her till she got crisp, then put her on
 a broken plate.
And I'd bring her to the office so
 the principal would eat her
and get a stomach
   ache.

 The children listened with wide-eyed fascination to this troubadour of violence, and when she was done there was a standing ovation. The excitement of her anger was heady stuff. And it opened up a discussion of a child's-eye view of the restraints to pleasure which authority places along the path of growing up. It is a perspective that clearly relates its level of resentment to how fair the restraints seem to be. Cathy's teacher's blind disregard of her rights, her arbitrary impositions on Cathy's life, her lack of sensitivity to her needs make this eight-year-old girl murderously furious. The bitterness that children feel at having so little choice, so few options, of having to be so totally dominated by someone else's orders is tremendously deepened when they perceive no justice in those orders that *are* laid down.

Even family commands often seem tyrannical to children, and bitterness lingers as the image of themselves as submissive serfs is reinforced. It is an image that binds their writing together when their anger is shared in a collaborative poem. It is to be called simply "Orders" and Jimmy begins it by saying:

"*Jimmy!* Don't talk with your mouth full!"

His mouth has barely closed on the line before the next child speaks—then quickly the next, and the next, while the poem turns into this:

> DO . . .
> say hello to my friends . . .
> go to bed . . .
> eat your meat. . . .
> COME HERE . . .
> and take out these garbage cans . . .
> and take your punishment like a man. . . .
> STAY THERE!
>   when I tell you to. . . .
> DIDN'T YOU HEAR ME
>   when I called you?
> CUT YOUR HAIR! You look like a girl. . . .
> You're a girl

WEAR A DRESS!
You look like a SLOB!
You smell like a PIG!
Sweep out this MESS!
You do what I *tell* you to. . . .
Who do you think you're *talking* to?
CLEAN . . .
the basement . . .
your face . . .
your shoes. . . .
WASH . . .
your hair . . .
your feet . . .
your hands. . . .
GET ME! my briefcase. . . .
BRING ME! my sewing. . . .
Clear the table. . . .
Set the table. . . .
Don't you know what side the forks go on? . . .
DO IT AGAIN!
DO IT RIGHT!
STOP!!
GO!!!
NOT YET!!!!
NO!!!!!

I listen and my head bobs to their ever-racing rhythm of resentment and constraint. I stop the carrousel, too exhausted to let it continue. (There's fuel enough to keep it running for hours!)

Actually, the anger children feel about arbitrary rules is intensified by the suspicion that giving or depriving them of pleasure is sometimes based more on adult need or mood than on what's best for them. In their lack of self-esteem, many children I talked with sullenly wondered, for example, whether their parents' bundling them off to camp every summer had more to do with grown-up summer fun than with their own. . . .

"My mother gets so excited," Nancy says acidly. "She goes on a diet and buys new clothes, and I hear her making all these dates with friends because she'll have 'more free time with the kids away. . . .' " Nancy's voice trails off angrily as she mimics her mother's cheery response to the summer separation, which Nancy herself has, at best, very mixed feelings about. Yet in spite of the irate suspicion that her mother really wants to "get rid of her," Nancy's anger is relatively benign. For she knows her mother loves her and for the most part has her best interests at heart. So, as Dr. Irving Markowitz explains, the family's "history of altruism" affects how angry a child becomes when altruism temporarily falters. It is only in those relationships where children consistently meet whimsical and arbitrary thwarting of their rights and self-respect that the dissonant sounds of rage may reach fever pitch.

To the degree that a child does feel uncertain about his life's relationships, he will know another, darker side of anger, that tormenting, esteem-eroding feeling we call jealousy. Childhood's need for parental love, for acceptance by other children, for respect and understanding by teachers and caretakers makes any competition for these responses extremely threatening. Many children, encouraged by nuclear-family exclusivity, clearly seem to feel that the acceptance of someone else automatically means their own rejection. . . .

"I hate it when my baby sister sits on my mommy's lap. I wish I could pinch her nose so she can't breathe and then she'd turn blue and then Mommy would think she was dead and would put her in the cemetery where Grandma is." So ends Eric's unabashed tale of hostility and wish for revenge toward the newborn infant who has infiltrated the family after Eric's four years of total rule.

But it isn't only life-changing new brothers and sisters who nourish rancor. Often it's older children, like Greta's brothers, who in their overpowering presence seem to create such unfair competition for her parents' attention. And many children of divorce are also grimly threatened by a parent's new romantic interest, even if every effort is made to have the child feel that his own place in love's circle remains firm. Sometimes a similar uneasy rivalry extends to other family members, as when a grandparent or favorite relative suddenly welcomes a new relationship into his previously child-centered life. Frequently it's an older brother or sister whose wandering affection makes jealousy bloom. Jimmy, for instance, has always had a particularly warm relationship with his eldest brother, the twelve-year difference in their ages making the older boy more parent surrogate than competitor. One Monday morning Jimmy announced that over the weekend his brother had become engaged. Enthusiasm did not color his voice as he described Sunday's celebration. And later that morning, he wrote this small story, so large in its tale of emotional conflict:

I felt happy and angry when my brother got engaged, and I also felt very sad. I kind of like the girl he got engaged to, but I feel like I'm losing him as a real good brother. I mean he's a real good person, and now he's good with his girlfriend more than he's good with me. I know that he still likes to be with me whenever he can, but I don't know anymore how much that will be. I really want to tell him I care about him, but it's kind of hard to tell that to your brother or to anyone. I guess she tells him, and maybe that's why he likes her more than me. I don't know what I'll do when he gets married. I think we won't ever be together anymore. I hope he waits a long time to be married. Maybe she'll get tired of waiting and will go away.

Whether jealousy spins the plot of violent retaliation we heard from Eric or the wishful thinking described by Jimmy ("she'll go away" instead of "I'll make her go away"), the fact is neither child can do anything to shift the scenery or change the cast. And this is true of every aspect of a child's anger. For while an adult can deal with his frustration by ridding himself of its source (quit a job, move away, divorce a mate), a child has no such options. He can only run in place, with anger nipping at his heels. A situation that sometimes, sadly, makes him direct his pent-up feelings against the only "safe" target—himself.

Yes, like the crib-bound baby who bangs his own head in frustration, some older children will pummel their own spirits in anger. Susan's jeering comments about her looks— "Aren't I *gorgeous!*" said with a sneer as she prances around in a too tight bathing suit—are clear evidence of anger turned inward. And even more serious symptoms of being the target of one's own anger may be seen in the child who compulsively gets into trouble or is continuously "accident prone."

On the other hand, the child who does wish to strike out rather than turn his hostility inward must often find very indirect ways to do so. Without the power to give full vent to angry feelings, he learns to be quite Machiavellian, showing resentment through deviously ingenious behavioral statements.

When Judy is angry at her parents, for example, she sucks

her thumb, a regressive behavior they find enormously irritating. Each annoyed glance they send in her direction makes the slurps more ostentatiously juicy as triumph gleams in her eyes.

"I say I don't feel like eating my supper when I'm mad at Mommy," Robert says, "even if I'm really, really hungry!" There's great pride in his voice at having found one small way to compensate for his inadequate strength in what may seem life's power struggle. No question: if it distresses his mother for him to go without dinner, a gnawing stomach is a price he'll gladly pay for the sweet taste of revenge.

Similar settling-the-score schemes can be seen behind all kinds of ostensibly innocent behavior. Particularly when deepened helplessness forces a child's anger even further underground, it may pop up again in a variety of deceptively innocuous disguises. So the child who whispers when the teacher is talking, just loudly enough to distract her, may be as hostile as the child who openly defies her. And the little girl who "forgets" to give the sitter an important message from her mother can be gleefully avenging, even though she's so meekly obedient while the sitter is in charge.

Still, while schools and teachers and friends and baby-sitters are all part of the collaborative story of childhood anger, it's inside his home and with his parents that the story becomes most complex. As the first place a child learns frustration, and where his emotional involvement continues to be greatest, anger will naturally be more potentially intense here. How that potential develops, however, relates to several interpersonal elements in the family atmosphere.

Anger is more evident, for example, in homes where parents are so concerned about standards of "good" and "bad" that a child grows guilty about hostile feelings. Anger is also unwittingly encouraged by parents who don't let the emotion die a natural death. An angry child who's behaved inappropriately is sometimes too long reminded of his "sins." The desire to make *sure* he's repentant causes some parents to maintain their disapproval until he feels demeaned and deeply resentful. An unhappily graphic example of this was given by Nancy, when she wrote:

"When my father gets mad because I've yelled at him, he never yells back. He just nags and nags and nags and nags. It's like he's hitting me in the head with an ax so I can't think because every time I try to think my mind bleeds."

But if persistent recriminations breed bleeding anger, inconsistency in standards does so as well. The "All right! *Have* another cookie" kind of exasperated parenting, where rules of behavior are worn down and thrown out for a temporary respite, promises an angry future even if it quiets negative expressions here and now. The child whose temper tantrum is rewarded will have a temper tantrum soon again. The permissible space alluded to earlier must be defined and maintained if a child's anger is to be successfully contained. Indeed, such consistency proves to be a much more significant factor in controlling anger than the strictness of the punishment if the child loses control.

Most important, however, in helping children deal with their hostility is to understand its inevitability. Dr. Jersild says that "children cannot develop normally without becoming angry." This is an idea that should diminish the grownup desire to sugar-coat the sometimes bitter taste of this part of a child's emotional life. For anger is indeed a life tool, beginning in infancy and continuing through the years. Though encouraged by helplessness and dependency, it is also, as noted, a statement of self, proof that this growing person cares about himself and about his life, and is willing to think deeply and defend developing values. However a child is taught to convert the feeling of anger into socially acceptable expressions, he must be allowed to acknowledge that the feeling exists. This kind of permission gives him custody over himself and promises that no matter how many times he must apologize for certain angry acts, he will not feel the destructive need to apologize for a very deep and significant part of who he is.

7/ Dreams

MY DREAM

All the walls had eyes
and noses like people
and they came after me
and I ran into the kitchen to
look for Mommy, but she wasn't
there, and the refrigerator had
eyes too and it started chasing me and
I ran into my room and jumped into
my bed and the bed started to run
and it just kept hitting the walls
with me in it and my head was hurting and hurting.

Greta's shouts woke her mother. Quickly Mrs. Walters hurried into her daughter's room to find the child sitting up in bed, a terrible look of fear on her still sieep-covered face. Eyes that shone so brightly during the day were now glazed and unfocused, looking backward into the world of darkness, a world children chart in the often blazing, often terrifying colors of their dreams.

Greta had been dreaming, she sobbed to her mother, of coming home from school on the last day of the term to go on a family vacation. She'd hurried down the few streets, "all excited," but then when she came to her block, everything was very quiet, and the car wasn't in the garage, and nobody was home. Greta's voice rose shrilly as she continued the night's story. ". . . And I went into the kitchen, and there wasn't any note for me on the refrigerator like you leave sometimes, and then"—her voice reached a hoarsely high pitch, threatening to crack entirely under the weight of her tension—"then I opened the closet to hang up my coat, and nobody's clothes was there except mine. And I ran outside and then I saw our car all the way down the street moving away, so I got on my bike so I could chase it, but . . . *all the wheels came off!*"

The last line was delivered with a wail of despair that pierced her mother's heart with its obvious revelations of how the child viewed her life and its relationships. Mrs. Walters is a woman with a fairly sophisticated understanding of psychology and a great empathy for her daughter's emotional experiencing, and she could hear the complexities of the legend Greta had constructed in her dream. She realized it was a tale rooted in the six-year-old girl's feeling of inadequacy compared with her older brothers and in the struggle, which seemed to her so hopeless, to win her fair share of their parents' attention.

Hearing her daughter's dream reported, Mrs. Walters had indeed been put in contact with the raw material from which its story was spun. And even if she might not necessarily have been entirely accurate in interpreting the dream's symbols, she'd been completely correct in recognizing that *through* these symbols, Greta was expressing some deep con-

cerns and conflicts. Actually, such recognition is not unique
to our sometimes self-consciously psychoanalytic culture.
For example, a tribe called the Senoi, who live in the Malay
Peninsula, have been the object of much study because of
their practice of regularly and openly interpreting family
dreams, including the children's. Every morning at breakfast
the child, along with all other family members, discusses his
dreams, and is directed toward actions meant either to affirm
or contravene the dream's message. Senoi people believe that
the images inside a dream reflect how a child is viewing and
adapting to the outside world. Thus, they feel, if the dream
images are negative, and the child keeps them to himself, he
may eventually suffer varying degrees of mental illness or at
least unproductive amounts of anger or aggression. Encouraging him to express his dreams, they conclude, lessens
this possibility. But the Senoi carry their dream validation
even further. They teach their children quite specifically to
act in ways that will detoxify the negative dreams and reinforce those that are positive.

This means that if a child dreams about an angry shouting
fight with a friend, he is told to seek his friend out that day
and speak to him lovingly—perhaps even offer him a gift.
Conversely, if during the night he dreamed of doing something heroic, he is encouraged to corroborate the dream
message by creating something that will truly help the other
members of the tribe. Stanley Krippner and William Hughes,
psychologists who have studied the Senois and dreams in
general, report that this particular group of people claims to
have very little violence or pathology among its members.
Whether or not this can be proved, clearly, the doctors say,
"from an early age the Senoi finds that others accept the
feelings and thoughts of his inner life."

This is unfortunately not at all so in our own society. Inherent to this book is the idea that we tend to avoid the rawer formulations of our children's concerns. However, just *because* of this, it becomes particularly important that we listen to the voices of our children as whispered in their dreams. If much in a child's waking experience separates him from his instinctual and emotional self, his dreams can serve as a way of integrating these factors into his total personality. As he falls into sleep, the floodgates open and a host of feelings and fears and impressions tumble forth in all their disorder and half-formed conclusions: feelings and fears and impressions and conjectures that in waking life, for a variety of reasons, he is likely to repress. A maternal frown when he begins to express a concern, for example, can instantly end a discussion not only with his mother but also with himself. Indeed, no matter how warmly welcoming the family actually is, or how receptive to all kinds of emotional confusions, the pressure of life's routines makes extended speculation about feelings and needs almost impossible. The momentum of daily demands catches child and parent alike in its no-nonsense grip, and there is little time for recognition of those tentative wisps of developing thoughts.

In his dreams, though, the child can confront them, and sometimes think them through. Calvin Hall, a pioneer in the study of dreams, called dreaming "thinking that occurs during sleep," and research continues to validate this aspect of the dreaming concept. Yes, a child's dreams are (as Freud postulated they were for all people) a protection against the build-up of buried emotional conflict. They serve as a safety valve to release the pressure accumulating from the never-ending input involved in growing up. But they are also, we now realize, a blueprint *for* growing up; a way for children to "process" all that they see and hear in the course of a day. While he sleeps, the child can roam around through the history inside his memory cupboard and try and make sense of it. He can go over the contradictions, the sanctions and restrictions of his life and, through the imaginary dream experience, get to the heart of a waking problem. Like the travelers on the road to Oz, the young dreamer wanders along a fantasy path to the root of the mystery that lies in his own unconscious.

In his dreams, then, a child experiences himself and his ever changing world. But it is a world that is deeply personal, far more concerned with feelings than with objective events. Dr. Hall reports that even during extravagantly dramatic periods of world history, dreams tend to be much more intimate than global.

So children in the midst of war or chaotic political activities do not dream about the material that makes the newspaper headlines. Their dreams contain instead the stuff of personal diaries—what they think about themselves and how they see the conflicts of their emotional lives.

In this vein, Dr. Irving Markowitz, who works extensively with children and their dreams, sees children's dreams as being particularly "prospective," as opposed to an adult's frequent use of the dream to engage in retrospection. As we grow older, we tend to look backward in our dreams, to review and reminisce and come to terms with our yesterdays. Nostalgia visits us during the night, just as it does with misty-eyed frequency during the day. Children don't dream retrospectively, because there's little material yet for nostalgia. Nor is there enough intellectual development to evaluate past decisions. No, from the very beginning of life, children are oriented toward the future. Childhood is presented as a prelude to being, "being" subtly synonymous with being an adult.

Also, children are, as we have said, painfully aware that the present, like the past, is still not in their hands. And they know they are inevitably growing, developing, moving toward a time when it will be, a possibility that, with their current feelings of inadequacy, blankets soft beds with the harsh cloth of anxiety. For these reasons, although both adults and children use the dream as a "work sheet," children make special use of its planning aspects. The challenges of days yet to come, still shrouded in mystery, are mulled over in their dreams. Sleeping, a child explores possibilities for action when darkness lifts, tests out the responses he might make to experience, along with the possible effects of those responses.

So it was that Judy, before she began kindergarten, had a whole series of dreams that unmistakably related to this larger-than-life event. In sometimes direct expressions of her worry: "I dreamed I got sick in the middle of the class and threw up all over the teacher . . ." at other times in veiled symbolism: "A lady came to the house and asked me a whole bunch of questions so I could win a prize, and when I didn't answer her she threw hot water on my face and said I would have to stay in the house for a whole year before the water could dry . . ." Judy dealt with the idea of leaving home. What if she refused to go . . . what would happen when she did go . . . what would happen if she got sick and needed her mother . . . what would happen to her relationship with her mother . . . what would happen if she couldn't learn as fast as the other children . . . ? These were all part of the night's conjectures.

Because of the particular planning function of their

dreams, children tend to carry their dream speculations to especially catastrophic heights. They will, considerably more than adults, explore in dreams life's most pessimistic promise. They will consider the very worst alternative rather than the most desirable one, with their speculations aimed at coping with the most traumatic trump card life may deal them.

This theory explains why so many of a child's dreams involve death or some other form of abandonment by a parent. Why, for instance, George dreams his mother "forgot him in a taxi," and Jason dreams his mother "fell on a knife and was cut all to pieces," and Robert dreams about being picked up in the mouth of a giant crab when he goes swimming with his father, so that he stays caught in one place while his father unknowingly swims steadily out of sight. These are all dreams that illustrate the depth of dependency that makes the idea of losing a parent's support so terrifying. Yet, through this imagining, strength can be gathered to deal with the awesome but inevitable letting go that is the goal of growing up.

Struggles with dependency are at the root of many of a child's dreams. Dr. Hall, in categorizing types of dreams, labels one large group "freedom versus security," and a child's nighttime conflicts regularly reveal this push-pull process. The safety and protection of dependency, the excitement and challenge of freedom competitively beckon the small dreamer, taking on many guises, but clearly expressing this classic life conflict. "I was going on a trip all by myself, but it started to rain so hard the plane couldn't take off. . . ." "I forgot my lines in the play and Mommy whispered them so loud that everyone heard them and I felt so embarrassed I ran off the stage. . . ." "I dreamt I was sleeping in my old room, in my old crib, and I was wearing my baby pajamas but my legs stuck all the way out because they were so small on me, and I was very cold, and then all of a sudden I got very sad, and when I woke up I still felt sad. . . ."

Not surprisingly, this kind of dream appears with special frequency at transitional times in a child's life. As in Judy's case, when starting a new level of school, or when going away to camp or becoming, with the birth of a new baby, an "older" brother or sister, the anxiety attached to growing up intensifies and reflects itself in symbolic dream arguments for and against maturity. Children faced with particular growing-up challenges will in their dreams struggle to feel competent to face those challenges. How to translate the work sheet's raw material into a working blueprint for what lies ahead?

There is a "rites of passage" aspect to this kind of dream, related to what psychiatrist E. Wellisch calls the struggle to find one's "way." Dr. Wellisch defines "way" as thoughts a child has about his "origins, tasks and aims." Dreams of a "way" often occur, says Dr. Wellisch, when the child senses he has "reached a significant stage in his way of life. He has to undertake a challenging task and, sometimes, to make a decisive choice."

A recent dream of Robert's serves as graphic illustration of this idea. It was a dream he awakened from in tears, but with a quietly resigned character to his sobbing that was very different from his usual dramatic howls of despair. It's a dream he remembers in quite full detail and is clearly, if painfully, willing to communicate. . . .

"I was being buried in a coffin, but I knew I wasn't really dead. A man told me (I *think* he was a nice man, but I'm not sure) that everyone who's seven years old has to be buried before they're allowed to be eight and nine and grow up all the way. He told me it was like going to school. You had to do it before you could be big. And I was scared, but I believed him. I knew that Mommy did it when she was little, and Daddy too. . . ." His face as he talked to me was taut with strain, and he seemed to need to have me understand its source completely.

"I knew I would be unburied after a while," he continued, "but I was still so scared . . . and I watched the other kids . . . my friend David who's in my class, and he was climbing into his coffin, and I was standing behind him on line waiting for mine—you know, like you wait in amusement parks for your car to come along the track and stop for you to climb in. I could see the coffin coming toward me, and the top opened up, and I had this terrible feeling 'cause I knew I *had* to get in. . . . There wasn't anything I could do, because if I didn't get buried, I couldn't be alive again. . . ."

Robert's voice trailed off, and he did not continue. Nor, in fact, had his dream continued. For these are the dreams that we would commonly label nightmares, those often terrifying battles with experience that abruptly end with a sob, a scream, a heart-pounding race to a parent's bed. Freud called the nightmare "a dream that failed." Dr. Markowitz speculates, appropriately to this discussion, that it may be rather a dream that cannot continue. If a child doesn't have enough history, experience and information in his memory cupboard to allow him to formulate an answer to a particular question, whether it be specific, like passing a test, or profound, like Robert's concern about meeting the challenges of maturity, he may simply have to wake up. For he cannot, on his own, finish the dream problem out.

There are other reasons, though, for the night's darker dreams, those that end too quickly or far too disturbingly.

The clash of impulses that are part of a child's learning to be a person creates dream scripts that are rich with conflict. So Dougie throws himself into his mother's arms after a nap. . . .

"I dreamed I was being chased by a tiger, Mommy, and she had *your* face!"

Heroically Dougie's mother comforts him, while she squirms uneasily at this confrontation with her little boy's repressed inevitable resentments.

Since such battles between hostility and love, or impulse and conscience, rage all through childhood, we can better understand not only the plots but the cast of characters who people its dream stories. The police and the convicts, the priests and the sinners, the angels and witches are often representative of a child's image of the different sides of his personality that will act out dramas heavily laced with guilt.

Actually, dreams also *contribute* to guilt, generating uneasy feelings that linger long after a dream has ended. For away from the external controls of waking life, a child will explore ideas in his dreams he would not ever consider acknowledging during the day. Because of this, he may use the bad dream as a way of punishing himself, as if, says Dr. Hall, "the nightmare is the price he pays for doing something wrong." So the punishing conscience shouts its accusations, and fills the dream with vindictive designs of retribution, like electric chairs and fires and furious principals and teachers; while lions and tigers and monsters quickly gain on leaden-footed dreamers.

These vengeful symbols illustrate the secret language of the dream. Symbols, the images of the dream, are the way ideas are expressed during sleep. The concept of symbolism is crucial to any discussion of dreams. But we have in recent years moved away from a strictly Freudian interpretation of these pictures in a dreamer's mind, which gave them rather categorical definitions. Today there is more inclination to see symbols as having individual meaning—in relation to the specific child's life.

Indeed, just because a child's dream symbols *are* so deeply personal, an attempt to respond to them can establish new levels of adult-child communication. Listening to the dream's revelations may give a glimpse of repressed frustrations, may allow parents to see that an ostensibly healed emotional scar is in fact still an open wound. For example, while Cathy was away at camp last summer, her parents had the family cat put to sleep. The animal was sickly and old and a nuisance to everyone but Cathy. Guilt over their legitimate but rather impulsive decision encouraged them to tell Cathy, when she came home from camp, that the vet had recommended the pet be placed in a country home for old cats and dogs. There were vague promises that they would take Cathy to visit her "soon." The story sat uneasily in Cathy's consciousness and, coupled with her longing for the pet's familiar place in her emotional life, she had many moments of really painful sadness. She wanted desperately to believe what she had been told but was unable actually to accept it. Yet fear and guilt and loyalty meshed into a complex conflict that sealed her lips. Till one night Cathy had this dream, from which she woke screaming:

"These people," she gasped, "they sent back a dog they bought because they didn't want him anymore. Then all of a sudden he was in like this big factory . . . and a man put him into a chopper and he came out in a bunch of chops like lamb chops and a lady with a bloody apron said I had to eat it for my dinner . . . and she told me to sit down at the table, and she gave me a knife and a fork, and she put the chops on this big plate in front of me, and it was all filled with blood . . . like soup! . . . and the *dog's face was there . . . it was part of the chop! . . . and the lady said go on . . . go on . . . eat it!*" Cathy shrieked this ending of her dream. It was too horrible to tell about, as it had been too horrible to dream any longer. And Cathy's parents, who had come to comfort their screaming daughter, realized through its grotesqueness that their protective pretense had been futile and that this nightmare cry was a cry for help in dealing with a terribly confusing life experience.

Dr. Markowitz, by the way, does not believe that parents should be hesitant about trying to decipher the symbolic code of their children's dreams.

"You don't have to have all the answers," he says, "to speculate, sometimes with the child, about what a dream might have meant to him."

Indeed, this kind of speculation can, with surprising alacrity, itself provide answers to some haunting problems. With Cathy, this meant that her parents, aware of their role in her distress, did their best to comfort her fears and explain her confusions. Bruce's mother and father made similar use of the dream to confront their child's raw concerns. During the period when Bruce was having problems in school, he had a series of sleep-breaking nightmares. The majority involved attempts to escape hideously ugly monsters or being hopelessly pinioned in their choking grasp. Finally, "although we tried to avoid the thought," Bruce's mother says rather ruefully, "we had to entertain the idea that not only was Bruce obviously really frightened about something, maybe we were in some way contributing to his fears."

With a little help they focused on the idea that there were

some "monstrous" binds in their son's life—monstrous defined as a situation he was helpless to change or control. Monster dreams often reflect exactly this kind of dilemma, although the dilemma itself varies from child to child. With Bruce it was simply the fact that an increased homework schedule was pulling at the rather rigid rules his parents maintained about an early bedtime. To a boy inclined to be rather plodding anyway, the constant tension only made him more so. So Bruce's dreams were a clear statement of the double bind his life had become.

Once aware of his problem, Bruce's parents relaxed some of the family schedules. Dinnertime was delayed a bit so that Bruce could get a good chunk of his work done before it began. In this way he didn't have the feeling of racing the clock from dinnertime on. Bedtime itself was also made more flexible, with his parents' sensible realization that it was far better for Bruce to sleep a little less than have his sleep broken with conflict-produced nightmares.

So Bruce's dreams became a communication tool within the family, a function of dreaming that becomes increasingly significant as dream research continues. One value of such "dream discourse" is that a child can express feelings he would be reluctant to confess in more direct conversation. Somehow the dream has a hypothetical quality that allows him to feel out his parents' attitudes, to try and gauge their degree of receptivity to a feeling or wish, without subjecting himself to the humiliation of the rejection a more open statement of self might bring.

An almost textbook illustration of this occurred between Jimmy and his father. Jimmy had been feeling particularly competitive toward his father, largely because his mother had begun helping her husband in his business and thus was suddenly away from home unusual amounts of time. Both adults were aware of the resentment Jimmy was feeling and also sensed the distress the resentment caused him, as he had always been particularly close to his father. Their sensitivity allowed them to hear the story of anger and guilt behind the dream story Jimmy loudly announced one morning, as he entered their bedroom when they were dressing for work. . . .

"I had this really awful dream," Jimmy said, his eyes focused on his father's image in the wall mirror. "It was about this scientist who invents a terrible monster, a mean, terrible monster. But the scientist was mean, too, and he used to boss the monster around all the time. So then . . ." Jimmy continued, his voice rushing now, words tumbling all over one another, "so then the monster one day sneaked behind the scientist when he wasn't looking and"—now Jimmy's eyes darted quickly away from his father's reflection—"and he punched the scientist on the head and said, 'Take that . . . take that . . . take that . . .' and he punched him until he was dead!"

An air of expectancy hung in the room in the few minutes before Jimmy's father, "acting on a hunch," made this reply:

"You know, Jim, I was dreaming myself last night. I dreamt you were all grown up, and had kids of your own . . . and I started to think how you might have children yourself someday, and how you'll probably try and do a lot of things for your children, but they won't always understand why you do them, or why you have to do other things they don't like at all, and they'll probably be really angry at you lots of times. . . . I remember feeling like that about Grandpa a lot, and I guess you must about me sometimes. . . ."

Father and son's eyes met again in the mirror. Without commenting, Jimmy suddenly turned and left the room, making his father frantically uneasy that he had "gone too far in my do-it-yourself analysis bit." But these fears were quickly allayed, for when he and his wife came down a few minutes later for breakfast, Jimmy was already at the table waiting for them, and waiting to add this addendum to their conversation:

"You know, Dad . . . about my dream . . . I didn't tell it right. The monster wasn't really such a *bad* monster, and he didn't really *kill* the scientist . . . he just kinda beat him up a little. . . ." The boy's voice trailed off and he turned his attention to his cereal, but it seemed very clear that a significant conflict in his life had been at least to some degree eased because he had involved his parents in the private world of his dreams. His father's obliquely empathetic response had allowed Jimmy to work some of his own feelings through. He was able to modify the harsher emotions that had made him feel guiltily murderous toward the man who had "created" him.

Validating the dream life of a child is not just an act of accepting who he is as a total person. It is also strengthening an extremely significant tool for structuring a life of greater enrichment. The kind of thinking that takes place in dreams is the kind that produces the highest level of creative thought. The magnificently bizarre combinations of ideas that take shape in dreams can produce profoundly creative results. Freed from the barriers of language structure and rules of logic, the dreamer can arrange thoughts into new patterns and experiment with the stuff inside his memory cupboard to see what variety of innovative conclusions might emerge. Dreams are flowingly open-ended, while daily life often closes in too quickly and abruptly for creative thinking to take place.

We tend in this culture to be wary of make-believe, and this extends to our feelings about night dreaming as well as daydreaming. Robert's mother listens to her son's breakfast recitals of the night's adventures and finds herself worrying whether he "dreams too much," as if his explorations into a private world are evidence of faulty adaptation to the public one. In fact, research supports the opposite conclusion. There is a correlation between dreaming during the night and learning skills during the day. The child who can think in images is capable of grasping complex ideas put into words. Say Drs. Krippner and Hughes, "The creative thinker typically accepts and exploits his dreams and the creative elements of his inner experience."

Many children I worked with kept "dream diaries," delighting in sharing their entries with other journal keepers. Listening to them, it was obvious that curiosity soars as the night darkens. Recesses of the mind's darkest corners are suddenly lit, illuminating all kinds of otherwise buried secrets of self. As Nancy writes, to sum up this chapter for me:

> Dreaming is like you're lying on
>   a raft
>   on a blazing hot day.
> Reflections of you shine off the water,
> And you float through them, so that
> all around you
> are pieces of
>   yourself.

8 / Shame

*"Everybody laughed at me when I said
the teacher's name wrong"*

The dictionary has a varied set of definitions for the word
"shame." Synonyms range from embarrassment to mortification to humiliation. The experience of shame is described as
a loss of pride or self-respect; a sense of being ridiculous,
indecent or unworthy. Clearly, there are many nuances to
this feeling, and clearly, too, they are part of the unwieldy
baggage children carry with them through childhood, bang-
ing against legs trying to catch up with experience, and
leaving bruises that throb with physical and psychic pain.
Even the dispassionate dictionary consistently relates pain to
shame, and any work with children quickly validates this
connection.

The hurt of shame is inevitable to a self still in formation.
For self-esteem will periodically suffer all kinds of blows as
certain experiments with freedom end in disaster. . . .

"I tried to cook my own breakfast and I dropped the pan
on the floor and I burned a hole in the tile and Mommy woke
up and yelled at me and said I could never turn on the stove
again," Judy says one morning. Her voice is ragged, her eyes
are averted, her self-confidence is obviously submerged under the burning taste of failure.

125

Erik Erikson, in his theories on identity, links the feeling of shame with the feeling of doubt. The child who is too often shamed by his failed attempts to stand on his own feet can begin to doubt his ability ever to take that stance. Indeed, one of the great dilemmas of growing up is how to emerge from childhood's natural helplessness without still feeling too incapable, too inadequate ever to handle life on your own. Children are so predisposed to thinking themselves incompetent that any condition emphasizing that perception, such as feeling ashamed, will vastly deepen their distress.

No matter how rapidly a child grows physically, secretly shameful feelings of smallness and weakness often pulsate inside, and these feelings must be hidden from sight at all costs. The fear of looking "stupid," of feeling "silly," of being "mocked out," are malevolent threats hovering darkly on the horizon. No wonder, then, that expressions of shame invariably connect the feeling to the idea of exposure. Ashamed, a child wishes to bury his face in the covers, hide in the closet, run away from home. In his dreams, he runs naked along school halls unable to find shelter, looks down when reciting to see pants fallen to the ground, goes to parties with all the wrong clothes on. Asleep or awake, there is the sense of being pinned down under the harsh light of a judging "other," derisive laughter swelling louder and louder around flaming ears.

Not surprisingly, we get this representative image from Robert, his face flushed with emotion, who says:

"It's like your skin is all ripped off your body . . . peeled away in big pieces, and you gotta cry and cry and cry, like Mommy would if she peeled a million onions."

And then Andy, who has reflected a minute on Robert's analogy, adds his own, clearly similar conception:

"Being ashamed is like your head is cut open by a big piece of metal like I saw in that sheet-metal factory we went to with the class . . . and the whole inside of your head is all hanging out."

To be made painfully visible, then, in all their inadequacy, revealing their incompetence and confusion for all to see. If such negative perceptions of self are natural to childhood, and we know they frequently are, shame about that self being seen is aggravated by the way we tend to relate to children. We are often more ready to fix blame than to teach responsibility, and we sometimes exhibit an unlovely predilection for "shaming" as a way of controlling a child's behavior.

Again, nowhere is this distorted interaction more evident than inside our schools, their atmosphere rich with possibilities for learning the pain of mortification, for being taught the guidelines of self-contempt. These are feelings, by the way, not easily checked into school lockers when the day is over. As Alfred Adler writes, many children grow up "in the constant dread of being laughed at," and he goes on to say that ridicule of children "retains its effect upon the soul of the child, and is transferred into the habits and actions of his adulthood."

There is no doubt that if "nothing succeeds like success," nothing reinforces a fear of ridicule more than being made to look ridiculous. Robert's anxiety about his coordination as compared with that of other children can be traced in considerable part to the humiliating mornings in kindergarten when he couldn't tie his shoes, those mornings when his teacher quite frequently, after heaving exaggerated sighs, would call out to some other child in a tone of abject weariness meant to imply (as it unmistakably did) utter disdain for Robert's incompetence, "Will someone please come up and tie Robert's shoes for him so we can go outside for recess? He can't seem to do it for himself yet." And there Robert would stiffly sit—no recourse but to face front—toward tables lined with jeering faces, hearing the barely suppressed giggles, the stage whispers behind loosely cupped hands. There he would sit while some better-coordinated classmate, sometimes a boy, sometimes a girl, would bend over him condescendingly and tie his laces into a bow.

The mortification of those days is beyond even Robert's gift for metaphor, and I would not think of encouraging him to attempt its description. To see his face when he merely begins talking about the experience makes me want to move on quickly to other things, suspecting even as I chatter about a current TV program that he will long retain the memory of those terrible mornings when he first learned the shame of competitive failure.

Jules Henry, talking about our educational system, says that schools teach children how to hate other children as well as themselves. The child who ties Robert's shoes preens in her superiority. Her success is built on Robert's failure, a very common pattern, according to Henry, in the way children are socialized, particularly as they become "educated." As for Robert, the perspiring after-school bouts with his laces did eventually lead him to master a skill. But the rewards of his accomplishment were joyless, because he was motivated not by the desire to succeed at a new challenge but to avoid the ignominy of disgrace. Henry calls this life's "essential nightmare," and goes on to explain that too often, "to be successful in our culture, one must learn to dream of failure," and of course all the humiliation failure brings.

It should be noted here that an aspect of oppression is to reject the person for the very qualities which define him. In other words, the Jew is persecuted for his Jewishness, the Negro for his blackness, the woman for her "womanly" qualities (such as intuitiveness or emotional intensity). Similarly, children are continuously attacked in schools for being "a baby." The contempt attached to the term is fodder for the child's own contempt for himself. Asking a child to do more than he's physically or emotionally able to do and then disparaging him for his helplessness teaches him to be ashamed of who he is, as well as undermining what he feels capable of becoming. He enters school with the limited ego resources natural to his age and then encounters shaming situations which will further inhibit his ego development. Not certain of who he is as a separate person, should he fail to conform to the teacher's perception of who he should be, he becomes ashamed of his own instincts and needs. So, in a hopeless spiral, his shame makes him feel *more* helpless, *more* inferior, less capable of ever meeting the teacher's expectations, less willing to let her catch sight of the vulnerable creature he really is. No matter how carefully books were studied the night before, the fear of making a mistake seals lips tightly shut when answers are asked for.

Not only in its oppressive demands, but also through the constant criticism that's so often a function of the role of teacher, does the school become a particular arena for experiencing shame. In a cartoon strip by Charles Schultz, dealing with the marvelous Peanuts gang, Lucy is saying in disgust that she is going to quit school once and for all, that "yesterday one of the teachers criticized my lunch. She said I had too many doughnuts and not enough carrots. . . . It's time," Lucy then says firmly, "to quit . . . when they even criticize your lunch!"

Unfortunately, Lucy's self-assertiveness is not the norm

for most children. Instead they tend to burrow deeper into feelings of inadequacy, internalizing more and more the teacher's negative judgments. Jason provides this ideal illustration one morning when we are walking in the park: I have my hands in my pockets, and he slips one of his own hands in alongside mine so that our fingers touch. It is a warm and pleasant feeling, but after a minute, Jason makes this comment, obviously reminded of some recent hurt:

"You know," he says bleakly, "my teacher makes me *feel* like a pocket, that's got all the wrong things inside it!"

The pocket was frequently used by children as a symbol of being ashamed—both because it was a place to hide and because it suggested the dark despair of the emotion. Similarly, when we would draw pictures about feelings, shame was invariably colored black, no light softening it, "as if," writes Beth, captioning an all-black canvas, "as if you will see so much dark that your eyes may never see light again."

One of the residual benefits of doing the research for this book was that some light did enter the darkness of shame when children shared the secret of it through their writing and talking. Eyes widened at the realization that they were not alone in experiencing the stings of embarrassment. Harry Stack Sullivan once talked about the "delusion of uniqueness," the feeling that we are different from each other and therefore somehow inferior. So when children bravely volunteered, "I wet my pants the first day of kindergarten . . ." or "Daddy makes me wear baby galoshes in the snow and everybody laughs at me . . ." or "I'm in a special reading class where everyone is stupid . . ." they could begin to feel the strengthening intimacy of being like each other and lessen the alienation of feeling so shamefully "different."

The push toward being like everyone else, to find some

identity in belonging, is, we know, very great in childhood. This is why, once again, school can produce so much material with which a child may begin building an apologetic structure for who he is. The simple dividing up of children into groups that define capability can quickly define the extent of their inferiority. So traditional schools that "track" their pupils or are particularly competitive athletically may be launching children down roads they'll have great difficulty ever leaving. And no matter how many ostensibly compensatory skills a boy or girl may have—being a good athlete instead of a student, or vice versa—if they are too deeply ashamed of their failures they will get little comfort from their success.

Feelings of shame for his inadequacies are fanned by any relationship that doesn't allow a child to take himself seriously as a separate person. The view of the child as an adult's property contributes unhappily to this destructive condition. No matter how the "property" is coddled and loved, the role is demeaning—and it is bitterly resented by the children themselves.

Instant heat, for example, is generated by the word "cute," to express an adult's affectionate feelings for a child. It seems the ultimate put-down, distressingly patronizing. Similarly, ask a group of children what grownups think of them, and the answers are rapid and angry. . . .

"Dumb . . . puppets . . . jerky . . . silly . . . like a toy . . . a plastic doll . . . stupid . . . a pet, just like a dog or cat . . ." Rage rises with each person-denying adjective, until finally, inevitably, the ultimate resentment: "We might as well be invisible."

The concept of invisibility was used over and over again by children talking about the shame of insignificance . . . like

Andy, who, after a classroom scolding, says angrily:

"My teacher sucks me up like a vacuum cleaner till there's nothing left of me to see that she doesn't like." And Susan, after being summarily ordered to wear an outfit she hated for a special family occasion, wrote this self-pitying but graphic poem:

> I talk and no one hears me . . .
> I touch and no one feels me
> Unnoticed
> Unheard . . .
> I'm invisible . . . not a person
> I'm not alive . . .
> So I must be a ghost . . .
> And my life is not a life, just
> A made-up story—
> *A horror movie!*

Invisibility was also used in children's writings to indicate a wish for protection, so that nobody could witness the humiliation of a mistake, in either dress or speech or behavior. At the root of either use of the symbolic image—anger at not being noticed, the desire to hide from critical attack —is the fact that children are inordinately concerned with what other people think of them. Uncertainty about self makes validation by someone else enormously important. As a child grows up, he is constantly tormenting himself about interpersonal relationships: will he be accepted, will he be liked, will he mess things up by doing something wrong? . . .

"I worry all the time!" Cathy wails. "When I'm with a bunch of kids I feel like I'm in a play, on a stage, and they're

the audience, and I'm going to make a terrible fool of myself. . . ." Beth nods her head in understanding and says, "I
know. Me . . . I guess it's more like I feel I'm a puppet, and
I keep taking me apart. I worry so much whether each piece
of me is going to work that I forget how to put myself
together. I just lay there in a lumpy pile and can't do anything."

Self-consciousness seeps through every day, and sensitivity
to any kind of disapproval is intense. Lack of self-confidence
makes every action a cause for trembling concern. Judy cries
herself into throwing up during Christmas vacation because
she is afraid her new haircut is too short and everyone will
make fun of it when she goes back to school. (Many did.)
And Robert comes into his class one morning shivering from
the cold, but when this grade's empathetic teacher asks him
where his sweater is, he says he forgot to bring one. Later
that morning, the teacher noticed a bulge in Robert's pants
that seemed unusual, and when she looked up again, a strip
of blue wool was peeking out of his pants leg. Before she
could unobtrusively call him to her desk, a classmate's eye
followed her own and in a few minutes poor Robert had once
again become the object of group derision. Hating the
sweater for being too "babyish" (it had a nursery design and
was quite short), he had stuffed it into his pants so as not to
have to wear it. Memories of shoe-tying days filled him with
tension about not seeming as mature as his classmates. Unfortunately, his solution backfired and trying to save face
ended instead with his face again flushed with mortification.

It is terribly painful for a child to step outside the circle
of sameness that can quiet his ever present fear of being
laughed at. To be "weird" or "queer" is quintessentially
awful and fear of the label paralyzes the child with self-

consciousness. One study of teen-age boys and girls showed that 52 percent became terribly distressed when even a stranger seemed to be "staring" at them. (And they were quick to give this interpretation to the most casual glance in their direction.) Immediately these children squirm under the imagined scrutiny, check zippers and buttons, straighten hair nervously; often they will leave a subway car or room because of the real torment involved in feeling appraised (knowing as they do, in all their insecure unknowing, that they'll surely be found wanting).

No question, much of the tension involved in being a child is deeply aggravated by shame. Life's relationships are strained, and children alternate between self-demeaning campaigns for approval and defensive withdrawing for fear of disapproval. They limit their experiences because of worry that they won't be able to handle new demands or will be criticized for making the attempt. And worry about being liked keeps pace with self-denigration, for it is the rare child who consistently greets himself with approval.

The concept of "ideal self" is very much present here—that discrepancy between what a child thinks he should be and what external and internal mirrors tell him he is. While the internal mirrorings of self are of course more complex, reflections in actual mirrors can cause their own very intense distress. Once the middle years of childhood are reached, this kind of problem is particularly acute.

As in Susan's case, often the problem is overweight. The tension-releasing comforts of chocolate and ice cream, plus the body's natural changes, pad adolescent forms with hated excess pounds. On the other hand, being skinny brings its own pain, especially when the bosom remains childishly flat while other girls' figures are taking on a sensual new shape.

As for the skin that is most visible, on the face, the blemishes of acne can blister the soul. No ointment will be overlooked that might clear a pore and each new product commercial is received like a promise of salvation. And what of buckteeth, or braces . . . or noses too short or too long . . . or eyes too small or pale, or myopic? The litany of shame is endless.

As we have already indicated, the lack of self-love touches other kinds of reflections. For not just how they look but how they act troubles a surprising number of children. . . .

"I have this real awful laugh," Jeremy says heatedly, as if he is confessing some long hidden perversion. It was Jeremy who had initiated a discussion about what we like least about ourselves. It is a discussion that amazes me in its shame-structured distortions of my objective view of these children. Now Jeremy continues in his ruthless self-analysis: "I sound like a horse. I make these gulping noises and sometimes I have spit in the corner of my mouth."

He closes his eyes in disgust as other children admit, with varying degrees of apology, their own harsh assessments of self in the world. . . .

"I clump around like some dumb cow," Bruce says. "I'm always tripping over things. I wouldn't dance with a girl for a million dollars—I'd probably break both her legs. . . ." "I always ask people for help," Lisa quickly breaks in. "I never make up my own mind about anything! I'm surprised I don't ask what I should make in the bathroom!"

Nobody in the group laughs. This is, each person knows, as serious a conversation as they are likely ever to have.

A good part of this social awkwardness relates to child-hood's intellectual limitations. Children are enormously concerned about "knowing what to say." They are so afraid that they'll say something foolish and be ridiculed *for* their limitations. Over and over I was stunned by the discrepancy between children's creativity of expression when they didn't feel they were being judged and the tight-lipped, tight-gripped hold on language when they felt that they were. If this last perception occurs in the presence of adults or older children, it also often plagues them in the presence of their peers. "Shyness" is revealed like a shameful scar when boys and girls talk about themselves. Lisa, for instance, draws a picture of herself lying on an ironing board, and says contemptuously, "This is me talking to a boy. Every time he talks I get stiffer and stiffer, like his words are ironing me flat!" while Bruce says, "I store up all my words like I was a container instead of a person, and I only can talk when I'm so stuffed up they have to burst out."

So the self-conscious child, in the company of anyone but trusted friends, and in any new social situation, approaches conversation with stutterings and stammerings and oppressive silences and nervous giggles, and their humiliating sounds and no-sounds ring in his ear long after the school dance or picnic or party is over.

If many parents don't realize the extent of their children's feelings of shame, they're often equally unaware of how much they themselves may unwittingly contribute to the feelings. It is a collaboration with self-consciousness that often begins at the very beginning of the parent-child relationship—on that day when the proud mother or father supplies the new baby's name for a birth certificate. For an amazing number of children are quite seriously unhappy about their given names. One study had 44 percent of the interviewees distressfully critical of their parents for not being more careful about the names they chose for them.

Thus we find girls like Beth shortening longer names out

of hatred for their "square-o" old-fashionedness, while Greta mumbles her name when asked, sure she'll be teased because it's so "funny" (read "unusual"). Bruce despises his name, which he sees as "faggy," and resents his parents for not having realized its rather elegant overtones would cause their son some embarrassment when he grew older.

And mothers and fathers as people—not just as occasional abusers of parental authority—are the cause of much discomfort to their children (who feel tainted by their relationship to adults who are subject to criticism). Studies of children's attitudes toward their families show that a great percentage are frequently "ashamed" of how their parents act and live. Mothers and fathers who dress "too sexy," who get drunk at parties, who act "gross" by being too sloppy or loud make dependent children ache with conflict. Love for parents mixes with shame for their behavior, and guilt rises, deepening the torment. And if children worry how their parents look to their friends, they worry as well how their parents treat their friends. Even very young children sulk over a playmate being ignored. . . . "Why didn't you smile at Jamey?" Dougie asks his mother angrily when she picks him up at nursery school. "She'll think you don't like her!" Similarly, rudeness, lack of sociability, arguing in front of visiting friends (just like they weren't even there!) make children cringe because of their accountability toward companions whose approval they want so desperately to maintain.

There are many defenses to cover the feeling of shame, not the least of which is a false bravado. Very often the swaggering, most competitive child is really the one who feels least confident about his own worth. Conversely, some children retreat almost permanently from social and competitive contact—hoping perhaps to announce their self-sufficiency but in reality making themselves inaccessible to the people who, they secretly know, would reject them if they met.

Too much shaming as a way of socializing a child can make him determined to get away with as much as possible in secret ways, as well as teaching him to use shaming as a weapon in his own relationships. Jason screams and writhes in the barber chair so the barber can't cut his hair, and Jason's father embarrassedly takes his son home, locks still long. Earlier that morning Jason had been punished, and now, clearly, it was his father's turn. Similarly, adolescents' "freaky" clothes are often, says some psychological theory, a way of shaming parents by vivid public rejection of the parents' values.

There is impotence in shame, whether it is used against others or burns inside the self. And it is an impotence that has at rock bottom a loss of dignity. Children, painfully aware of their powerlessness, are acutely sensitive to any reminder of their weakness. As a child, this growing person must ask for, be given, permission, entreat; daily, in a dozen ways, humble himself. Resentment burns deeply when that unavoidable condition of childhood is in any way exploited.

" 'Please,' " says Jason, "is the worst word I ever heard," and his implication is clear. It is an implication adults would do well to remember when they deal with children whose dependency should not obscure their rights to a sense of dignity about their developing selves.

9 / Sexual Feelings

Mothers have eggs inside them and daddys take off all their clothes so they won't get dirty and then they help the mommys cook the eggs so they turn into babies. . . .

JASON

If this book is dedicated to the idea that children should be allowed to tell real, not mythical, stories with their lives, the stories should be free of a censor. They should not be cleansed of the lusty, swirling sensuality that is so much a part of childhood's emotional experiencing. For the truth is that from their very earliest days babies exhibit behavior that can only be called sexual. The sucking on breast or bottle brings gratifications quite apart from the pragmatic food-getting goals of the act. A baby's tongue and mouth and lips are tools for sensual explorations that dominate his attention as he sucks furiously, face reddened with concentration. . . . And when the hunger abates, and the sucking slows down, there is a look of contentment on the perspiring face that tells us other appetites, too, have for a little while been sated.

Yes, how something tastes, how hard it is, how soft it is, how cold or how warm, are filtered through oral membranes and translated into perceptions that may, according to some views, affect the kind of total person the child will become. Even in these days of questioning the absoluteness of certain Freudian theory, there seems to be general agreement that children who have been seriously frustrated in "oral gratification" will know a considerable amount of interpersonal anxiety when they grow older.

Babies are also, in their rich sensory experiencing, acutely sensitive to odors. In this period of animalistic pleasure-seeking, they live much of their lives through their sense of smell. Long before a child recognizes his mother's face, he is familiar with the scent of her body, a scent that may vary with her emotions and so evoke different emotional responses in him.

Psychologist Richard Krebs has written about babies who respond to their breast-feeding mother's sexual arousal in another room. Suddenly, as the woman turns to her husband, the baby wakes from sleep in apparent hunger. The doctor speculates that the sexual arousal of a nursing mother releases the milk from her breasts, and the baby, so sensitive to her smells, is awakened and calls out (competitively?) for her attention.

That there is a sensory and sensual pleasure in the smells of the baby's own body is very evident when he plays in his crib or playpen. He is, for instance, not at all disgusted by the contents of his full diaper—quite the opposite. He likes and is stimulated and pleasured by its warm, moistly pungent odors.

And later, cleaned and powdered, this still primitive new person will show other signs of sexuality. Dougie's mother, for example, remembers being horrified the first time she found her then infant son with an erection. Yet the fact is that babies frequently have erections; one study of nine infants from three to twenty weeks showed that seven of the nine had at least one a day. And each incident was accompanied by observable tension and release of tension, clearly related to an adult's more sophisticated, but no more meaningful, sexual response.

That children's erotic life *is* meaningful is too often overlooked by the adults whose attitudes so influence their lives. Indeed, perhaps in no other area of relating to children is there more denial and condescension than toward their expressions of sexuality. To some extent this complacency allows parents to accept more easily the sexual experience of masturbation. (It's relatively simple to be tolerant of something you don't take seriously.) So when Judy comes shrieking into the kitchen one morning: "Mommy! I found a button inside me just like the elevator button at Grandma's house, and when I push it I go up and down inside!" her mother can smile benignly without an earlier generation's disapproval. (On the other hand, later that morning Judy overhears her mother repeat the story to a friend, and the amusement in her voice makes the little girl's face flush with confused discomfort.)

In reality, a child's body contains nerve endings and organs of touch that make her highly susceptible to tactile stimulation. So no explorer could know more excitement than Judy can, and did, and does from her unexpected clitoral discovery. There are, of course, differences between children's capacities to be sexually aroused, but every child will experience some part of the sensual continuum and know the delicious pleasures of stroking, rubbing and prodding their own genitals. Many children have experienced orgasm even before the age of five, and clearly they did not have to know the name of the feeling to know how good it felt.

Children, however, *do* vary in their sexual development, and that they are pushed by the myth of innocence into one sexual pattern is the source of serious individual conflict. The boy or girl who is sexually "precocious" often suffers severe emotional pain. For our morally ambivalent society is uncomfortable with the child who is "too mature," whose body seems inappropriately developed for her chronological age. . . .

"Put something else on," Cathy's father says before the family goes out for dinner. "That sweater's much too tight on you." Cathy stares at him and flushes in embarrassment. And in her room when she yanks the sweater over her head, the swellings around her nipples disgust her. She is, after all, only eight years old, and if five years from now breasts will be prized, today they are despised symbols of her being "different."

Adults' uncertainty about sexual norms affects all of a child's sexual experiencing, precocious or not. Even with masturbation, which may be intellectually accepted by parents and other adults, residual resistence often appears. An uneasy sense that he'll be "overstimulated" has parents poking into the child's private meetings with himself.

In actual fact, masturbation is generally more soothing than exciting, which is why from infancy on it is usually indulged in at bedtime. The hand between the legs under pajama or nightgown slows down the story of the day's adventures, and helps turn the page into sleep. When boys and girls write about nighttime feelings, invariably they reveal this soft side of sexual pre-sleep activity. . . .

"When I lie in my bed," writes Nancy, "I feel like my body's a candle, that flickers when I touch it . . . and feelings drip from me like wax. I hold on to my body while darkness hovers around and comes closer and closes in on me. I lie very still and touch myself and listen to the quiet, and soon I hear the wind rustling and the trees sound like they're whispering, and the wind blows out the flame and I cover myself with my blanket to stay warm, and I go to sleep."

And Beth writes: "When I lie down in my bed, I feel my body is lying in the middle of a brook. Feelings rush through it, as if over rocks and weeds, smoothing my edges and rough spots . . . shooting around the corners of myself until I feel washed all over, sparkly, silky clean."

Yet despite these poetic testimonials to the comforts of masturbation, Beth and Nancy and many other older children too often feel guilty about it. This despite the fact that as they approach adolescence they are moving into a time of ultimate sexual upheaval, a time when their sex organs will mature and there will be heightened demands to satisfy sexual urges. Actually, in cultures where boys and girls can experience each other early in life, the masturbatory experience is quite rare. In effect, it is our social system of extended childhood that forces the hand to find its own sexual release, and it is yet another irony of a child's life that he is made to feel guilty and weak and ashamed because of this culturally induced activity.

However, since we *are* a society that postpones heterosexual gratification, we quite naturally (if unnaturally!) recoil even more from sex play between children of different sexes. Since some aspect of such play is indulged in by every boy and girl, each "game" helps grind down the myth of the happy child. For the child who "plays doctor," or shows his when she shows hers, soon feels an uneasy element in his temporarily pleasurable tension. The sexual taboos in our ostensibly liberated world run very, very deep, and few children will escape their force. Impulse wrestles with a confused conscience over and over again, as the child tries to understand some very important human differences. . . .

"Look at that!" Jason says, awe-struck, as a classmate accommodatingly spreads her legs after pulling down her pants. He pokes her vagina gently, and gets down to see if he can see up inside it. His curiosity is pure and natural, yet when his teacher walks into the room he flushes guiltily and his friend hurriedly pulls up her pants, bumping her leg in the process. The teacher comforts her, and nothing is said about what she's just witnessed. Nonetheless, both children know, even if they don't know why, that this particular anatomical comparison elicits more grown-up attention than a comparing of noses or hair or height.

The forbidden elements of sex explain its frequent appearance in children's humor. For instance, Judy can't resist a play on words during a kindergarten game of learning colors. The children are instructed to clap their knees and identify the colors of their overalls. Around the room it goes: "blue knees . . . green knees . . . red knees . . ." The closer it comes to Judy, the more I become aware of some inner struggle taking place. She seems to be fighting off an insistent smirk. And the game continues: "yellow knees . . . brown knees . . ." and it comes to Judy, and she looks at her teacher just for a moment, and then at me observing in the back of the room, and she slaps her hands on her hips and shouts, "Hy-nee!" The class is overcome with laughter; ribboned heads are thrown back and chubby fists are thumped on desks in indescribable glee. Surely nothing this outrageously funny has ever been said anywhere else on earth. And surely, too, Judy has learned the power of suggestive language. She shares with her peers a new respect for words like BM and penis and duty and pee-pee and bellybutton. They are part of a young comic's repertoire, guaranteed to bring an anxious laugh from the audience.

And later on in life, the smutty story brings equally loud laughter from clusters of children huddling on the brink of maturity. In classrooms obscene notes are passed, filled with words whose implications are as uncertain as the French or Latin phrases they're supposedly there to learn. For children use humor as a mechanism for dealing with inner turmoils and confusion, which is why their humor is so clearly related to developing interest in the opposite sex. Alternating currents of desire and disgust at the idea of heterosexual sex are both responses from which jokes, nervously "dirty" ones, are made.

But before a child can deal, humorously or otherwise, with the issue of attraction to the opposite sex, he must first resolve the major question of what it means to be the sex he himself is. It's a question whose answer doesn't come ready-made at birth, even though the physical definition is of course there. Early in life, the differences between male and female seem obscure, and a child looks for concrete answers to help explain them. . . .

Dougie comes running into his house from playing outside to announce he's visited a neighbor and seen her new baby.

"How nice," his mother answers companionably. "Is it a boy or a girl?"

Dougie considers the question, suddenly troubled because he's over his head. But then a light flashes across his face. It isn't his fault that he doesn't know the answer. . . . "I couldn't tell," he says brightly. "It didn't have any clothes on!"

To Dougie it is clothing cues, not parts of the body, that tell boy from girl, and his approach to the question illustrates the thinking of the young child. It is too often ignored that children's thinking about the meaning of sex roles is totally different from adults'. "Boy" and "girl" are labels they vaguely know are pasted on their bodies, but when they look in the mirror of themselves, the label's meaning is elusive. So it is that before three years of age, most children will be inconsistent in their answer to the question "Are you a boy or a girl?" and will comfortably play mommy *or* daddy in games of make-believe. Even at four, children will still feel that if you changed your hair style or put on a dress instead of pants, you could become the other sex, and that mysterious future when they will be grownups seems wide open in gender possibilities. . . .

Jason comes running into the kitchen after his father scolds him. He grabs his mother around the knees and buries his head in her lap.

"When I grow up," he says, voice rich with emotion, "I'm going to be a mommy—not a daddy!"

While Jason's vow of course relates to the moment's anger toward his father, it represents, too, the instability in his understanding of sexual difference. So although his mother greets this declaration of love a little uncomfortably, her concern is needless. For the fact is that it will be a while yet till Jason understands that boys remain boys and girls remain girls, and his confusion simply reflects his stage of conceptual development.

By the time children are five, they *do* generally understand the constancy of sexual identity. But the conflicts attached to that perception remain and continue as they grow. For example, despite a relaxed cultural attitude toward homosexuality, many children in the middle years of childhood are terribly worried that they may be homosexual. This anxiety is related to and also complicated by the fact that homosexual feelings, and even experiences, are very common at this stage of development. Indeed, not only are the feelings psychologically natural, but knowing the self-doubt of these years, they are almost inevitable. How can you not admire, envy, covet the beauty of another boy or girl who seems to have escaped your emotional and physical blemishes? But when you do admire, when you do admit to the secret feelings, what torment there is, what terrible secret shame at this irrevocable proof of not being like everyone else, of—oh, ultimate negative label—not being "normal."

Too often the sharp stabs of accusation are public and, however unjustified, may leave many lingering scars. Last year Susan was brutally ostracized by a segment of her school for her obvious crush on a class leader. This other girl was everything Susan herself would want to be—slim, blond, skin smooth, body firm. As she stroked her silk comforter, Susan hungered to touch this girl's overwhelmingly perfect surface. One day, as she was worshipfully standing near her in a momentarily empty classroom, Susan did exactly that. But at the moment her hand made contact with the other girl, a gaggle of students bounded through the door. Susan froze, and her fear was quickly seized on by the crowd and molded into ugly epithets—dyke, lesbian, queer. Crimson, crying, Susan pushed through the group and ran home, screaming to her mother that she would never go back.

Of course, in the powerlessness of her childhood, she did go back, did take the jeers and the abuse, and although her mother talked to her and tried to help her understand that her sense of disgrace was inappropriate, her suffering continued, further eroding her struggle to build a coherent sense of herself. A fragment from Susan's journal from that time proclaims her pain. . . .

> There goes fat girl
> answering a fire
>   inside herself.
> The flames erase the twisted picture
> she . . .
> calls . . .
>   me.

Ironically, while many children like Susan show newly accelerated homosexual concerns, other children encounter the problems involved with an accelerated exposure to heterosexual experience. For if we are a culture in transition, young people have often already arrived at brand-new places on the sexual map. And so boys and girls are often torn between the behavior of their peers and their parents' older set of moral codes. In Tommy's camp last summer, among the campers his age, there were secret underground strategies for an elaborate "bunk fuck." Tommy was ripped with ambivalence. . . . Should he go, shouldn't he go? Ultimately the plans were foiled by an alert camp director. But not before Tommy had written this entry in the journal that he, like Susan and so many other children, keeps religiously:

> The ax of suppression chops at my feelings
> until I'm too weak
>   and afraid

to
scale my parents' barricades.

Studies prove that the pressure to perform heterosexually at earlier and earlier ages is creating, as it did for Tommy, very real problems for great numbers of children. The "sexual revolution" has made unwilling revolutionaries out of far too many boys and girls who in the name of liberation have lost the freedom to say "not yet." Adolescent pregnancies are escalating crazily, while growing numbers of girls as young as ten will turn off an already precocious introduction to the menstrual cycle by becoming pregnant.

And that pregnancy doesn't occur doesn't only imply abstinence. Susan and Nancy and almost every other child I interviewed who had reached the junior high school level casually referred to girls they knew who were "on the pill." Yet these children also revealed, as indeed did their sexually cavalier friends, an uncertainty about sex as troubling as their parents ever knew in their own pre-pill childhoods. Sexual intercourse often serves as a poor substitute for the emotional intimacy really being sought in a relationship, and bodies too often behave in ways unrelated to minds and emotions.

Sex contributes to distress also by the way it can reinforce fears of personal inadequacy. As we've seen, children are constantly measuring themselves against one another and, particularly in this aspect of their self-perceptions, are quick to find themselves wanting. The agony in locker rooms and summer-camp bunks will be intense when the penis which always seemed too small clearly fails the competitive measure, and barely budding breasts seem even flatter next to the swelling bosom of a friend.

The desire to find sexual definition makes almost any part of sexual development a cause for competition. Beth, impatient to begin menstruating, watches her calendar with the concentration of a criminal marking off a sentence—doomed, she feels, to the prison of her childhood while all around her other people are escaping. She pokes herself every night in the bathroom, hoping, hoping to see the toilet tissue tinged pink. Each pristine white strip of paper convinces her she is headed for unwanted medical celebrity—the first girl to go through life never menstruating.

But even as Beth hungers for female validation through menstruation, other girls, like Susan, already padded or tamponed, often seethe with self-consciousness too. Susan's menstrual flows are heavy, and when she stands up in a classroom to recite during those periods, she is flooded with fear. What if a bloodstain has appeared on her skirt? What if the bulge of her padding shows?

Boys, of course, are not immune to concerns about sex-related public exposure. The erection that takes sudden command of tight jeans makes Jeremy double over with emotional pain when the teacher calls on him—pain as real as if he'd been physically struck in that most sensitive part of his body. He feels a terrible shame at being so out of control—a shame that keeps him from engaging his parents in the kind of discussion that might clear up his complicated-by-confusion distress.

Certainly no writing about children and sex can be complete without touching on the distortions their own writings often contain. Whether it's about erections or how babies are made or are born, a child's image of sex is colored by his inability to grasp certain sexual concepts in their entirety, as well as by the emotions those half-comprehended concepts quickly ignite.

Nancy and a boy go skinny-dipping on a dare and their bodies briefly come together underwater, and Nancy, despite an ostensible knowledge of reproduction, spends many sleepless nights convinced she's pregnant. And Jason, who believes babies are hatched from king-size eggs similar to the smaller ones he saw chickens lay on his uncle's farm, freezes with terror when a very pregnant woman takes a seat alongside him on the subway. His mother, standing over him, cannot understand the abrupt change in his mood—doesn't know until much later that Jason was sure the baby would burst out during the bumpy train ride, forcing his own involvement in the—to Jason—not at all blessed event.

And if children are bewildered about themselves as sexual people, they are equally perplexed at the thought that their parents relate that way to each other, or indeed to other men and women. No matter how legally divorced, the mother who comes home from a date flushed with sexual fulfillment can enrage a waiting child. The anger may not be articulated, even to the child himself, but clearly and unhappily it is there. And working with children of even the most properly married parents shows how mind-boggling the idea is of parental life behind closed bedroom doors. To relentless questioning by Jason, for example, about how babies got *in* their mothers' stomachs in the first place, Robert finally, in tremulous voice, answered that mothers and fathers "take off all their clothes and lay on top of themselves."

Robert and Jason stared at each other in sudden silence— Jason trying to make sense of the image, Robert trying to deal with the feelings finally saying *it* out loud had started swirling. Minutes passed and I watched Robert's face, unwilling to intrude in whatever he was working through (even though I sensed his parents would soon be drawn into some clarifying discussion). Finally his face cleared. It was obvious he had settled something in his mind, and now he helpfully passed it on to Jason, who was patiently waiting for his older friend's considered wisdom. "I guess that's why you and me don't have brothers and sisters, because our mommys and daddys didn't like doing that!"

Jason giggles, and Robert grins, and the conversation for the moment is over. What is significant in this discussion is the way in which Robert, out of his reluctance to see his parents in a sexual light, created his own mythology about their sexual behavior. Clearly this is reminiscent of how adults deal with the similar wish to avoid the truth of their children's sexuality. Partially our procedure stems from the way we have repressed our own childhood's sexuality. Partially it is because we continue to aggrandize the myth of innocence. Neither reason is reason enough to continue the pretense that our sons and daughters are not sexual people, for as long as we cling to that deception, children will wander in puzzled circles of feeling, perhaps having to deny aspects of themselves that will permanently impoverish relationships and their lives in general.

childhood, is overwhelmingly profound. Love places a warm hand on a child's back, guiding him through the often wintry winds of development. Over and over, research proves it is indeed the certainty of love that steadies childhood's step and provides enthusiasm for the rest of life's journey. One study, for example, of 158 "well-adjusted" children (that is, children with no really debilitating problems) concluded that the significant shared quality of these comfortable-in-life young people was that their parents were clearly devoted to them and, more importantly, the children knew they were.

And here, of course, we have love's rub. . . .

For if parents and children inevitably have difficulty hearing each other across the gulf of disparate perceptions, the interpretative gap is widest in respect to the ways adults give and children perceive "evidence" of being loved. It's a problem far more complicated than the difference in the development of cognitive powers. We are talking now about need and the imbalance between a child's appetite for parental love and his parents' ability to satisfy it. Psychologist Alice Rossi points out with a simplicity which belies the problem's dimensions that a child's need for mothering is "absolute," but even in the best of relationships the need of a woman to mother is only "relative." While this truth has always been with us, today it is particularly so, as more and more women try to combine mothering with some interest outside the home.

That closets lined with baby food and diapers are not exciting enough to all mothers to warrant shelving other needs until their children grow up does not of course mean they feel less love for their children. Clearly, many devoted mothers also engage in careers. But the situation does underscore Dr. Rossi's point about the different emotional requirements of mother and child.

It should be pointed out here that "mothering" can often come from fathers. As sex roles become redefined, parenting, too, expands its patterns and emotional responsiveness is less and less limited to biology. But whether it's mother or father (and obviously one would hope it's both) who through affection can bridge the gap of discrepant needs, there are times in childhood when the gap will yawn to an apparently un-bridgeable width. In these developmental phases, the child is like a ravenous diner at a banquet, gobbling up every proof of caring—the affectionate touch, the affirming word, the welcoming smile. . . .

"Mommy was so happy to see me when she came home that she started to cry!" Robert says one morning while he shows the class presents his parents brought from their European trip. And the lilting pride in his voice clearly says it was those tears, not these elaborate toys, that are the homecoming's real gift. Robert's entire being is ignited by the glow of love returned. His self-esteem soars through reinforcement of the idea that he is important to the people so very important to him.

Because love's well-being is so total, it's understandable that much children's writing about love involves all their senses—how its presence feels or looks and sounds. Remembering that children are afraid of loud and sudden noise, we can appreciate these descriptions:

"Loving is soft and gentle and quiet," writes Beth. "Clocks make tiny tickings and all the sounds in the house are just hums and everything you touch is like blue velvet."

Jeremy, too, uses a sensory framework, but this time to make a connection between love and self-discovery. "Love makes different kinds of quiet," he writes. "There's a soft silence where you can think anything you want to, and let your mind wander without having to stop it. I like to do that because even though I'm thinking a lot of things, I can rest."

Jeremy's description, through its suggestion that the child secure in love is free to discover himself, illustrates how love unfolds the fabric of self-awareness. Encouraged and appreciated for who he is, he can roam about in his mind to see whom he would like to become. Dr. Irving Markowitz explains that the uncertainty a child feels about his own productions, whether they're goals or feelings or ideas, makes him need immediate response to his efforts at every tentative step. Dougie wanders away from his mother with big-boy bravado when they visit the playground but he returns to her bench in a little while and pats her on the cheek, and receives her hug with a satisfied giggle. His swagger is a little more certain when he leaves her again, for in that affectionate interchange was what has been called "emotional refueling," the self energized by the strength of love.

Similarly, Beth calls her mother at the office to tell her about a test score, while Greta stares hard at her father as she lets go of his hands and pedals off herself on a new two-wheeler. The pride in the children's independent achievements expressed in Beth's mother's voice and on Greta's father's face encourages, as nothing else can, more and more experiments *with* independence, as well as giving the push to develop further intellectual and physical skills.

Studies of children's intellectual development invariably support this conclusion. Once again using the dramatic extreme to illustrate a point's general significance, children who are really love-starved by their natural mothers show enormous acceleration in learning when given continuously tender and stimulating surrogate care. One six-year research project, for example, involved twenty-five "emotionally disadvantaged" infants. Their lethargic dullness caused a scientific projection of a high probability that "they would slip to an IQ of 85 by the age of six." When outside stimulation was provided, by consistently available and affectionate "teachers," the children steadily brightened. Apathy became alertness, passivity stirred and was transformed into resourcefulness. By the age of six every child was reading, and all tested at the "superior" score of 125 to 130.

Obviously the children involved in this book are not similarly deprived and so will not be exposed to the potential tragedy of a stunted intellect. But even with the accepted, economically and emotionally advantaged child, there is a direct relationship between the loving presence and the push to learn. A paper delivered at a recent psychiatric meeting on this subtle interplay concluded that "children who later grow up to be exceptionally competent intellectually probably do not become so because of innate capabilities only." Starting almost in the cradle, the authors of the paper said, "these children have daily experiences in their homes which selectively promote their intellectual development."

The "experiences" referred to didn't mean only how many "educational" toys a child has to play with, or even how much physical time his parents spend as learning-play companions. Presence is indeed important, but presence alone can be more frustrating than nurturing. Judy, for instance, once angrily told her mother, who was restlessly participating in a game of checkers, "You have your back in front of your face!" Thus, at a very early age, children can recognize the difference between dutiful eye contact and real engagement.

Of course, all parents will have moments when they are less than absorbed in their child's chatter or play, but as long as children see the more constant reflection of love such moments will pass without serious emotional incident. It is these steadier images that contain the concept of "reflected appraisals," that process through which a child's idea of how his parents feel about him affects how he feels about himself. Not only do positive appraisals promote self-confidence, they also teach a child about the more profound aspects of a love relationship. When Judy's mother leaves a note on her pillow that night, telling her how much she loves her, and that she's sorry she spoiled her checker game, Judy learns something about generosity and forgiveness. The next morning she tells her mother that "when I have kids I'm gonna say what a sweet mommy you are sometimes." However conditional Judy's praise may sound, in reality she has gone beyond early childhood's totally selfish demands for love to an image of mature caring that she will develop and carry with her to yet another love-needing generation.

Judy's more realistic awareness of love's behavior points up a love-related problem that the mythic image of childhood engenders. Grouping all children together under one happy smile assumes that they have identical love needs. Yet children, as individual people, are actually quite different from one another in their temperaments. They will cover a vast range of emotional ground in both dimension of need and in the intensity of the demands they make on a relationship.

So Robert, who like Judy would like total commitment from his mother, complains bitterly when she goes to two meetings during the same week, even though she has never worked and is extravagantly available to him.

"You're *never* here when I need you!" he wails in deprivation as she leaves him with the sitter, and only awareness of her son's insatiability keeps her from feeling inappropriately guilty.

On the other hand, Beth is, as she has been since birth, enormously self-sufficient. In her baby carriage she would gaze endlessly at the hanging mobile as it swayed in the day's breeze. Now she reads several books a week, writes long passages in her diary, loves to do crossword and picture puzzles. Indeed, so much is the private-pursuit part of who she is that she told the camp director, when discussing summering at his camp, "Yes, all the activities sound very exciting, but I have to have at least one hour a day to be just by myself."

So Beth stands on the other end of need's continuum from Robert. Therefore, although her mother has a full-time job, and even though she does get worried sometimes about being physically alone, her security-giving view of her mother is that she is emotionally available to her.

Clearly, the comfortableness of the fit between parent and child relates at least in part to who the child constitutionally is. But it also relates to who the parents are—as individual people and, perhaps more importantly in terms of their children, who they are as parents. Men and women become mothers and fathers for a variety of reasons. They see the role as satisfying a wide spectrum of needs and behave in the context of that role in many different ways.

Studies that have involved ways of parenting all show that there is indeed broad variation in attitudes and behaviors. Some parents are "indulgent," others "democratic," some "coercive," still others "authoritarian." The correlation between a specific parental approach and a child's development is fragile at best. What's more, it is really academic. For the *real* issue is not which kind of parent is better or worse for a child, but that *for* better or worse, children are raised by the parents they have. Mothers and fathers should not feel guilty about this inevitable situation. Given the fact that we are all human beings, it's unreasonable to believe that another parent's strengths and weaknesses are any more balanced than our own. As long as we recognize our children as separate people, entitled to their own strengths and weaknesses, they will do equally well inside our particular family walls.

Children are of course aware that other families are not mirror images of their own, and are not above making sometimes critical comparisons, often to their own parents' discomfort. When Greta tells her mother about the other mother who "kisses all the time," maternal concern escalates. Should she be more affectionate? Used to older children, who periodically reject physical affection, perhaps she has not been attuned enough to Greta's needs.

Actually, Greta's mother has little reason to feel guilty. True, she is not particularly demonstrative, but she shows her love for Greta in innumerable ways. It is entirely possible that Greta was making only a simple comment, noticing differences that she hadn't been aware of when she was younger. Nonetheless, Mrs. Walters did try to show her affection and approval for Greta more actively after that comparative statement, and she feels, from Greta's behavior, that it was an appropriate response to have made. Certainly there is some validity in weeding out what might be a legitimate message in a child's reports about parental differences. It is not only in their dreams that children sometimes say things to their parents indirectly. However, it should be stressed again that, by and large, we are the people our own childhoods shaped us to be, and as long as we raise our children with good will and love, they will prosper accordingly. . . .

But they will also suffer, and not just because of our flaws or failings. Of course, there are many times when parents *will* be the cause of their children's pain, and we will continue to try and rise as parents above the character problems that make this happen. But no matter how successful our efforts are, our children will know, along with the exquisite joy, bursting hope and delicious excitement of their childhoods, a darker, more violent, bitter side of life.

The reason we have explored this side within these pages is quite simply because there seems no alternative, considering the world we have brought our children into. The flow of experience rushes around us, making it harder and harder to chart a course. The accelerated rate of change that is the dynamic of this time clearly demands that the mythical conception of childhood be challenged. Fantasy's child will not swim well in these unfamiliar currents.

The social pressures and tensions that command the attention of adults do not, no matter how we would wish otherwise, leave children unaffected. It is they, in fact, who are often most caught by the world's confusions. We are a society that too often maintains the idea of the child as property, a perception that allows us to work out adult anxieties and disappointments *through* our children. So as an athlete might groom a son to captain a Little League team, our culture pressures children to achieve in ways it calls important, and also to compensate for inadequacies it may now regret.

For example, postwar concern about losing ground to the Russians (called by psychiatrists "sputnik anxiety") resulted, says one psychological report, in a "breakneck acceleration of scientific curriculum" that was often "harassing" to the children it was imposed on. Similarly, these last transitional years have made children the vehicles of many grown-up struggles with social change. Studies of those troubling issues of "bussing" and school prayer conclusively proved that the needs and feelings of the children, in classrooms or in transit, were rarely important factors in agitation either pro or con.

We must abandon the perception of a child as "possession" if he is to learn how to take responsibility for his own life. And if children have always had to do this as they grew into maturity, it is a particularly important life goal today. For more than at any other time in our history, adults are becoming inadequate models for a child's socialization. As indicated at the start of this book, much of what we were taught to believe in and live by may not prove the most useful equipment for today's child. The old verities are not nearly so helpful as learning to feel comfortable with less rigidly defined behavioral directives. A child today must be flexible, unafraid of unknown challenge; above all, he must move more and more confidently into independence and autonomy. Children today must be choosers, who will not panic at the unlimited number of choices their lives will present them with.

They must, therefore, achieve the consciousness of self that will allow them to pause in order to choose, rather than be forced into behaviors that have little to do with their inner needs. A coherent plan of action comes from knowing who you are, and only a person who is encouraged to be whole can know this. If a child pushes part of his experience underground, he may become separated from parts of himself that are necessary to form the wholeness of the person he is becoming.

The myth of the happy child encourages children to repress and deny too much of their real experiencing. The impact and implication of feelings are left unexplored, even though these feelings make up their self's sense of place in the world. So it cannot be overstated that the myth of happiness imposes far too negative an imperative on reality's child.

There are other reasons, too, for dispelling the myth of the happy child—reasons that also relate to the child's search for a meaningful sense of himself. The wish to have our children always happy may prevent them from meeting some very necessary challenges. According to Dr. Irving Markowitz, and he is only one analytic voice out of many on this subject, it is impossible to find happiness in maturity if unhappiness in childhood isn't dealt with at least to some degree.

A childhood that was truly as blissful and carefree as the myth implies would mean the crucially important labors of development had not been engaged in. It would place the self in a hothouse, not where it should be, in the open air. Yes, the temperature of the hothouse is soothing, but it stifles the growing personality, so that, according to Dr. Markowitz, the "happy child" may turn into an emotionally stunted adult, bewildered and frightened and still dependent as he moves ill-equipped out into the cold winds of maturity. Thus not to allow children the experiential struggles inherent in growing up is actually a deprivation and makes the myth of happy childhood a mockery.

Allowing a child to accept the full range of his emotional life also teaches him the skills he needs in order to deal with life's emotional issues. One of the most crucial of these is learning how to be intimate with other people. Here, too, there is almost total professional agreement that a child who is not allowed to experience his real self will never be truly able to love or feel loved by someone else. Again, the myth of happiness plays its destructive role. A child who is ashamed of his feelings may believe he is not lovable as he really is. And so instead of seeking intimacy he will avoid exposing his true self, believing he would surely be rejected if he were ever really "seen." As if he were still a toddler in the playground, all his relationships take the form of a kind of "parallel play," where the people move gingerly around each other but never really touch—are always, barrenly, alone.

And, too, in excess the wish for a happy child leads children themselves to establish goals of happiness that are equally unrealistic and frequently damaging psychologically. If, as Arnold Toynbee once said, "Life is the voyage and not the harbor," being oriented only to the harbor can color the voyage dull and disappointing, with the rewards never grand enough to bring real contentment. There is a reason why Robert cries after opening his Christmas presents and why Cathy is sulky after a lavish birthday party. And the reasons are not totally related to their being overtired. Rather, the long anticipation of both occasions, the compulsion to reach ecstatic peaks while they take place, make reality (inevitably?) a letdown. Both Robert and Cathy soon become disgruntledly upset that they aren't happy "enough," and later Robert downgrades what he has been given (to localize the blame for his depression), and is already planning what "better" things he'll ask for when next Christmas comes around.

It is not cynicism but awareness of life's complexities that makes us know no gift exists that can reach the point on the happiness continuum Robert is pushing for. Happiness is not so easily manufactured, and it is perhaps this above all that should propel us to abandon a mythology that leads children to believe that it is. We must not raise children with an image of happiness that in its superficiality will ensure their being disappointed. In a sea of plenty they will then know only thirsty discontent. It is time for them to listen to and create other kinds of stories, stories grounded in real rather than fantasied experiencing, stories whose emotional tone is rich enough to grasp the intricacies of the plots life will continue to create, stories whose messages are significant enough to help them understand those other plot lines, even the ones whose narratives are upsetting.

Childhood is indeed a special time of life. But inside its special "place," a child should be allowed and helped—by his parents, his teachers—to discover his real, not his mythical self. After all, he himself is the most important element in his unfolding true-to-life story.

No one is more important in a child's life than his mother and father, but to use our unquestioned power gracefully, caringly, and to loosen our grip on it when it's appropriate, is the challenge of the parental role. At the same time, parents should rid themselves of the oppressive sense that they alone are responsible for a child's emotional pain, or that they could, if only they were better parents, get rid of those pains. Freed from the false mythology that generates such false guilt, they can help their children grow into authentically experiencing adults.